The FEAR-19 Pandemic

How lies, damn lies, and fake statistics created a pandemic of fear that spread faster and caused more damage than COVID-19 ever could have by itself.

Special thanks to my boss for the great job with editing.

Special thanks to my Hommey for the wonderful cover.

Preface

There are a literal, well maybe figurative, ton of references in the back of the book if you want to check my research or read the entire articles or scientific studies that are quoted or screenshot.

My motivations were to show you the science and psychology behind what took place during March 2020. The COVID-19 pandemic was terrible, but there were self-inflicted wounds that could have, no, should have been avoided.

There are a lot of screenshots from the media and scientific reports in the book. It was important for me not to just tell you but show you what took place.

Enjoy!

Table of Contents

Opening

While in the military, I served in an NBC (Nuclear, Biological, Chemical) unit. Those units are currently known as CBRN or Chemical, Biological, Radiological, and Nuclear. One of the functions of our unit would have been to clean up after an NBC attack. There are several things I remember about my time in that unit, and it had numerous effects on the rest of my life.

One of the things I remember is how hot it would get in those suits. You would be soaked in sweat in about 15 minutes, even less in the summertime. Hydration was critical. This information didn't affect my life much moving forward, but it was one of the things that stuck with me. Those suits were miserable.

One thing that did affect my life was decontamination training. You would go through an extremely regimented process of getting undressed after being in the field. And if you would miss even one small detail, they would stop and tell you that you just killed yourself, and everyone in the room with you. It was challenging, and I remember watching long time vets fail on their first try and have to repeat the training.

This contamination training taught you to carefully watch what you were doing and what others around you were doing. You developed an awareness of what was and was not contaminated. To this day, when I am out in public, I constantly see things that people are doing that are contaminating them. Not just during this most recent pandemic, but all the time. It's a bit annoying, and I try to ignore the thoughts.

Another training they gave us was desensitization training. In this training, we were shown picture after picture, or videos if they had them, of what germs, bacteria, chemical agents, and radioactivity would do to the human body. It was a lot of horrible stuff. The objective was to get us accustomed to seeing those effects, so we would not freak out when we were in the field.

They also taught us a lot about germs, viruses, bacteria, and the effects of radiation. We learned a good bit about these things and how they operate. The possibility of epidemics and pandemics, combined with discussions of 1918, 1957, and 1968 flu pandemics, was rather alarming. The 1968 pandemic was not as far in the rearview mirror as it is today.

Now, while all of this was excellent training, there were some problematic side effects. This combination of understanding contamination, recognizing how poorly the general public was at containing contamination, and all those images of the damaging effects from germs, bacteria, and viruses turned me into a bit of a germaphobe.

It wasn't just that I was uncomfortable in crowds; I had a difficult time using and then exiting from public restrooms. I mean, seriously, public restrooms are all just one big contamination. The worst is when some moron comes out a stall, rinses his hands off as if that would magically clean them, puts his contaminated hands under an air dryer creating fecal mist to share with everyone. Come on; he had flushed the toilet, so we already have that mist, did he really have to add to it? The idea of this fecal mist filling the room would make me sick to my stomach.

I have gotten better over the years at not letting all of this bother me so much. However, one of the lingering effects is that I am scared of pandemics. I know a big one is coming. It's not a matter of if, just when. It seems like a weird thing to be scared of, right. Well, I learned more about pandemics than most people, have the terrible effects of things drilled into my head, I understand contamination, and am keenly aware of how bad the general public is at avoiding contamination. We just will not be able to stop it.

My nightmare scenario is something as deadly as Ebola and as contagious as the measles. That will be apocalyptic.

So yes, I am one of "those" people. I have prepared for the zombie apocalypse: suits, masks, gloves, medical equipment, and food for a possible shelter in place. I started calling it the zombie apocalypse as a coping mechanism. Calling it that works because the concept is funny to me, which is better than just being anxious or scared. Plus, having prepared for the zombies is a comfort as well.

So, anytime something weird starts up somewhere, I will regularly read up on the emerging information to see if it's the "zombie apocalypse." My point to all of this is that I was paying attention back in the early part of January, when they were still calling this coronavirus a mysterious pneumonia.

And by the way, anyone concerned about a viral apocalypse has heard of Wuhan, China. I was laughing when they said it came from an animal market in Wuhan. Okay, sure it did. I am sure it had nothing to do with China having its virology lab in Wuhan. That lab's location is just a coincidence, nothing to see here.

Because I knew what was in Wuhan, I was a little more concerned than usual with this mystery pneumonia and was closely watching as information started to come out. Then, in February, the Chinese produced the first big study with statistics.

For the germ nerd who is watchful for the Zombie apocalypse, this report was great news. First, they were reporting a mortality rate of 2.3%. I realize that seems terrible, but the reason this was good news is that initial reports of mortality rates are always extremely elevated. There is always a lot they do not know, and as they learn more, these numbers **always** come down. Anyone who follows these things knows the initial numbers will drop.

The last pandemic to come through was H1N1. The early mortality rates on H1N1 were as high as 4-5% if I remember correctly, and it ended well below 0.1%. So, this one starting at 2.3% was great news.

The second major thing was that they reported 80% of cases were mild. This information meant that the virus was not that severe. For comparison, the flu has an estimated 75% asymptomatic rate. There can be a difference between mild and asymptomatic (no symptoms), so I knew we would need to wait for more information. But at first glance, this all seemed like good news; it was likely to be no more severe than the flu.

The last bit of good news was that the virus had little to no impact on children. That seemed unusual but was welcome. H1N1 was more destructive to children. The older you were, the safer you were. Now, the younger you are, the safer you are. Children being safe is good news psychologically.

Now, President Trump had already instituted his travel ban from China when this report came out. As a pandemic paranoid person, I was initially somewhat supportive of that ban. But, after seeing these numbers, the travel ban seemed excessive to me. This thing was just not going to be that bad. My thought was that Trump was still doing some hard negotiating with China and sending a message.

The Diamond Princess cruise ship was the next big domino to fall. The Cruise Ship presented a great opportunity because they would learn a lot about the virus from this little "lab."

On February 20th, the Japanese National Institute of Infectious Disease released results from the testing on the cruise ship. Those results included the following.

1. 20.6% of those tested were positive for COVID-19.
2. 51% of those cases were asymptomatic.

The term asymptomatic means what it sounds like, no symptoms, they were infected but not sick. The 51% was lower than the 80% of cases that China had reported as mild, but this was an elderly population averaging around 60 years of age, so it made sense. We already knew that the virus was more severe in the elderly so it would make sense that there were also less asymptomatic cases. Also, China reported those cases as mild, so maybe they just used different terminology. They could have had a similar number of symptom-free people.

The bottom line, those numbers did not have any alarming results as they fell in line with the information coming out of China. So, my zombie apocalypse radar was further relaxed; this was not the one.

Things continued to move along rather steadily and predictably for the next few weeks. Cases started popping up all over the world. But there was not anything that was really alarming to me.

And then, in the words of the immortal Ron Burgundy:

"well, that escalated quickly, I mean that really got out of hand, fast."

I am not referring to the coronavirus escalating. It seemed to continue moving at a steady pace, spreading across the globe. Instead, like Ron Burgundy was expressing, I am referring to how people just lost their minds. Fear, hysteria, and panic spread faster and more dangerously than the virus.

The Setting

There is a large segment of the population that has an intense dislike, more accurately, a hatred, for Donald Trump. This is not a partisan statement, just an observation. If you "oppose" Trump, you know what I am talking about, and you know how you and others feel about him. If you are a "Trumper," then you call it Trump Derangement Syndrome. If you are one of us who do not fall in either camp, you struggle to understand why everyone seems to be drinking "kool-aid." It's just some are drinking red "kool-aid," while others are drinking blue "kool-aid."

The bottom line is that Trump elicits strong emotional reactions. There is not much middle ground with Trump, one side loves him, and the other side hates him. I believe those strong emotional reactions were the key to why the FEAR-19 Pandemic spread faster than COVID-19 did. To understand why this happened, we have to understand the environment leading up to that time.

Let's begin with a discussion of the reasons the Trump-hating crowd cannot stand the man. Here are the ones I hear the most.

- Trump is a racist, a sexist, a bigoted xenophobe, and he embraces white supremacists.
- He is a corrupt liar, a narcissist, and a con man who bullies anyone who disagrees with him.
- He is mentally ill and dangerous.
- He ignores science and only makes decisions based upon politics or money.

I probably left some things out, but you get the picture. We are not going to discuss the merits of any of those beliefs. The point is just to identify these beliefs so we can understand why things rolled out the way they did.

We probably should add that they don't just think these things, they don't just believe these things, they **know** these things. As the oracle from the Matrix would say, "you just know it, through and through, balls to bones." They **know** these things about Trump are true.

Here's a snapshot from an article that caught my eye a while back, and I wanted to share. This article was released on October 19th, 2019, while the impeachment hearings for Donald Trump were proceeding in the House of Representatives.

"Mental health experts see Trump is dangerous, but our professional gatekeepers protect him."

President Trump is dangerous

Soon after the inauguration, I organized a conference around the ethics of speaking up about a public figure, and from it came a public-service book, "The Dangerous Case of Donald Trump: 37 Psychiatrists and Mental Health Experts Assess a President," a collection of essays from some of the most prominent psychiatrists and psychologists.

Our message was simple: The president was more dangerous than people suspected, would grow more dangerous with time, and could ultimately become uncontainable. Much of what we predicted in the book has come to pass: Trump's rhetoric has clearly incited violence, cruel policies against children that could lay the groundwork for future violence, enhancing a culture of violence both domestically and abroad, and the weakening of institutions that might have contained him.

This article is not some blog from the far corners of the internet. This article is from a Yale School of Medicine psychiatrist and published in USA Today; this is as mainstream as it gets.

This line of thinking is just one example of how hatred for Trump permeates our mainstream society and media. The media is even more disproportionately anti-Trump than the rest of the population. This statement is an observation, not an attack.

Turn on and watch MSNBC for an evening and tell me there is not a strong distaste at best, but probably more accurately, a hatred for Donald Trump within a large portion of the media. The media is not just biased against Trump; they have a visceral dislike for the man.

Just in case you are not sure about this bias, let me show you a few things. Of the top three network news (ABC, NBC, and CBS), the top three cable news channels (Fox News, CNN, and MSNBC) and the top three online news channels not listed already (NY Times, Huffington Post, and USA Today), eight out the nine are left-leaning according to Media Bias/Fact Check's online model. Only Fox does not lean left.

Still not convinced? The Pew Research Center released a study where they showed that during their first days in office, Barack Obama received positive coverage 42% of the time, Bill Clinton 27%, and George Bush 22%. In comparison, Donald Trump got positive coverage only 5% of the time.

Here is one more tidbit. Leading up to the 2016 election, journalists donated $381,814 to Hillary Clinton's campaign compared to only $14,373 to Donald Trump, according to publicintegrity.org.

While the general population is pretty split, the media is disproportionately anti-Trump. Now, remember, the Trump-hating crowd **knows** how bad Trump is and can explain these studies. For example, the fact that Trump only received positive coverage 5% of the time is because he is the worst President in history, so there is nothing positive to say. And well, the explanation kind of makes my point about how they view him.

Let's look at the core beliefs of this Trump-hating crowd in a logic chain.

1. Trump is a bad and dangerous man.
2. Trump does bad things that endanger everyone.
3. Because of this, we need to remove Donald Trump from office.
4. Until Donald Trump's removal, we should resist or oppose him at all times, so he cannot do as many bad and dangerous things.

Again, I am not arguing the merits of any of this; I am just identifying the beliefs.

During the Senate hearings in January, PBS released a poll that 85% of Democrats felt Trump should be removed from office. Keep in mind the disproportionate number of democrats within our media. From watching the media coverage, I would anecdotally say that the press was somewhere around that same 85%, if not higher. They seemed to believe that he should be removed and worked very hard to show everyone why.

There is another reason why the media is so blatantly anti-Trump. They see themselves as the fourth estate, so they feel it is their responsibility to counterbalance power. Here is a snapshot from an article on Medium.com titled: **"The Fourth Estate – on the role of journalism: Facts vs. Fake News"**

> The purpose, 'raison d'être', of this fourth element is to act as an counterbalance, a systemically opposite force that is to report, verify and question matters of governance, public matters as well as commercial ones, conducted by the powers, we the people, have entrusted it with and bestowed upon.

The Trump-hating portion of the media has this additional belief:

5. It is our duty to expose all the things about Trump listed above.

13

I am not arguing the merits of any of these beliefs, that is not the point. We just want to identify the mindset of a large portion of our society, a disproportionate percentage of media, and the politicians of the democratic party. I do not believe I have to spend even one second explaining how much the democrat politicians dislike Donald Trump.

Now, let's go through a few events from early 2020, and discuss how they impacted this Trump-hating group.

On February 5th, The US Senate voted to acquit President Trump on the articles of impeachment. This acquittal ended an extended storyline that had been playing out in the media. It began with the Russian collusion story that ended with an emotionally disappointing dud. They tried to give it legs with the obstruction of justice storyline, another dud. When that was going nowhere, they started on the Ukraine "quid pro quo" and abuse of power. In what seemed to me like an irrational desperate move, the House impeached President Trump for Abuse of Power and Obstruction of Congress.

That impeachment ended with his acquittal on February 5th. This moment was yet another anti-climatic dud. It is essential to understand the context of that point in time to see what happened next. The Trump acquittal was an emotionally charged disappointment for all those anti-Trumpers that added to a string of emotionally charged disappointments.

This dud left them with a bubbling cauldron full of disappointment, frustration, resentment, and anger. The pressure in this cauldron had been growing with each additional disappointment, threatening to boil over.

However, there was the election coming, so there was reason to hope. They could defeat Trump in the election, and finally, get him out of the White House. The media spent a good bit of time covering the Democratic primary contests in February. That was their lead story on most occasions

―

Along comes Super Tuesday on March 3rd. There was a lot of drama leading into those contests. It was coming down to a two-person race with the nomination up for grabs. Then, Joe Biden does very well on Super Tuesday, winning the majority of states and securing a lot more delegates. That day pretty much secured the nomination for Biden. It was not over, but Joe Biden was now the assumed Democratic Presidential Candidate.

The Huffington Post polled Democrats and independents who lean democrat just days after Super Tuesday. In that poll, they asked people which candidates they would be enthusiastic about, and they could choose more than one. The poll identified only 48% were enthusiastic about Biden. And 21% said they would be upset if it were Biden.

My theory is that this was just another emotional letdown. Simply put, Joe Biden does not inspire. I do not think his victory energized and provided hope about ending Trump's presidency. They may have wanted to believe that Biden could win, but I think in their collective subconscious, they knew he would lose. This gradual realization had to be disheartening, especially after the enormous emotional dud of just a month ago.

There was nothing left to provide hope for the Trump-hating crowd. This absence of hope added pressure to the emotional cauldron of disappointment, anger, and resentment. This was the emotional state for a large portion of our population, the democratic politicians, and a majority of our mainstream media at the beginning of March.

Plus, with the democratic primaries pretty much settled, a new lead story to create interest in watching the news was desperately needed as well.

The Prelude

Early after the shelter in place order went in effect in my area, I was at the grocery store to stock up on a few things. While getting some groceries, I was noticing the people around me. Everyone seemed so tense, scared, exceedingly conscious of not getting close to anyone, the fear and anxiety were palpable. My initial thought was, what is wrong with you all? This is not the one. This is not the zombie apocalypse.

At that moment, I realized how shockingly relaxed I was. I realized that we were suddenly in a Bizzaro world. That epiphany was kind of funny.

You see, typically, I am the uncomfortable one. People, especially crowds of people, stress me because I know they are all contaminated. For example, they lick their fingers before touching my grocery bag and my groceries and then ask for my card. Ugh!

Now everyone is hygienic. They are not crowding me. They are cleaning things. They have washed their hands. They are not trying to touch my stuff. It was heaven for the person who typically worries about those things. In the middle of a pandemic, I was more comfortable in public than I had been in a long time.

But it was also troubling because you could see the fear and feel the tension in the air. My initial derision was gone, and I began feeling bad for everyone. I was empathetic because I knew how they were feeling and understood how uncomfortable they were. Plus, while I had gotten better, this was all new for them. It was just sad.

This epiphany made me curious. Why was everyone so scared? This was not the one. I began looking into everything to see if I could figure out what was going on. It wasn't that I was trying to find out about the virus; I had a grip on that. I started looking into why everyone was so scared. Maybe I could help people feel better. Maybe I could explain why they could take a deep breath and relax.

That journey of enlightenment has brought us here. My goal is to explain how we all got to that point, so maybe, we can avoid the same mistake in the future.

In the last chapter, we talked about the emotional state of the Trump-hating portion of our society. Remember the core beliefs regarding Donald Trump using a logic chain.

1. Donald Trump is bad and dangerous.
2. Everything Donald Trump does is bad and dangerous.
3. We need to expose that everything Donald Trump does is bad and dangerous.

Let me give you an example of how these logic chains play out.

On January 29th, Donald Trump announced a Travel Ban from China to combat the coronavirus. Here is what how the logic chain goes.

1. Donald Trump is bad and dangerous.
2. Trump bans travel because he thinks COVID is a problem.
3. Banning travel is bad.
4. Thinking COVID is a problem is bad.
5. We must expose that COVID is not a problem so we can expose that Trump is bad and dangerous.

Here are some stories from the next three days.

- January 29th, NPR:
  "Worried About Catching The New Coronavirus? In the US, Flu Is A Bigger Threat"
- January 30th, US News and World Report:
  "Why the Flu Is Still a Bigger Threat to Americans Than Coronavirus."
- February 1st, The Washington Post:
  "Get a grippe, America. The flu is a much bigger threat than coronavirus, for now."
- February 1st, USA Today:
  "Coronavirus is scary, but the flu is deadlier, more widespread."

This shows how their logic chain works. Trump says COVID is bad and issues the travel ban. Media says flu is worse. They **know** it has to be because Trump is using coronavirus for his bad purposes.

Now, jump ahead a month to February 26th, at a press conference, Trump states, "I think you have to treat it (COVID) like the flu."

At a campaign event two days later on February 28th, he made the famous "new hoax" comment and again compared COVID to the flu.

And then the next day in the initial press conference for the Coronavirus Task Force, Trump makes yet another comparison between the flu and COVID.

And so now a new logic chain emerges.

1. Trump is bad and dangerous.
2. Trump is comparing COVID to flu.
3. Comparing COVID to flu is bad and dangerous.
4. We must expose that comparing COVID to flu is bad and dangerous.

That brings us back to March 3rd, Super Tuesday. During a World Health Organization (WHO) press conference that day, the Director-General Dr. Tedros Adhanom Ghebreyesus says the following during a draw out explanation about how COVID-19 is different from the flu:

"Globally, about 3.4% of the reported COVID-19 cases have died. By comparison, seasonal flu generally kills far fewer than 1% of those infected."

This quote gets some attention, but it's Super Tuesday, so the primaries soak up most of the spotlight. However, within the next two days, everyone is beginning to realize that Biden is going to be the candidate. The democratic primary story is winding down.

And on Marth 5th, Trump breathes life into the COVID vs. Flu story. While being interviewed by Sean Hannity, Trump states that this number from Dr. Tedros was a **"false number."**

Giddy up! The Trump-haters don't need to figure out how to make Joe Biden more appealing. All they need to do is get Trump, and they finally have their opportunity. Trump was defying and ignoring the "experts" by minimizing COVID. Trump thinks he knows more than the experts. Trump disregarding experts puts people in danger. With more focus on this story now, it begins to build momentum.

Next, Trump continued to feed the story himself when on March 9th, he tweeted the following:

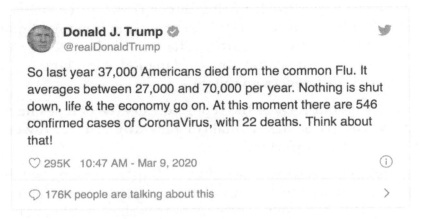

Donald J. Trump ✔
@realDonaldTrump

So last year 37,000 Americans died from the common Flu. It averages between 27,000 and 70,000 per year. Nothing is shut down, life & the economy go on. At this moment there are 546 confirmed cases of CoronaVirus, with 22 deaths. Think about that!

♡ 295K   10:47 AM - Mar 9, 2020   ⓘ

💬 176K people are talking about this   ⟩

Talk about poking the bear. Trump does seem to love poking that bear. The tweet got a good bit of attention.

The storyline continues: Trump is defying the experts, minimizing the dangers, stubbornly ignoring the science, and endangering us all.

1. Trump is bad and dangerous.
2. Trump is minimizing COVID by comparing it to the flu.
3. Minimizing COVID is bad and dangerous.

The next day on March 10th, Dr. Anthony Fauci, a member of the president's task force, went on the FOX News' Sean Hannity show, and stated the following:

"But Sean, to make sure your viewers get an accurate idea about what goes on, you mentioned seasonal flu. The mortality rate for the seasonal flu is 0.1 percent. The mortality rate for this is 2, 2 ½ percent. It's probably lower than that, it's probably closer to 1. But even if it's 1, its ten times more lethal than the flu. You've got to make sure people understand that."

Boom goes the dynamite! Even his own experts disagree with him and are correcting him. And it was on FOX News, Sean Hannity, to boot. Even the most ardent Trump supporter heard that. Trump is ignoring and defying the experts, and that puts us all in danger.

This moment was the convergence of the things we talked about in the last chapter:

- The hope for getting rid of Trump is restored as he has finally been exposed to everyone.
- The lead story has emerged. Trump is defying the experts, trying to get people killed.
- The cauldron of pent-up energy empties. All the frustration, all the disappointment, all the anger, and all the resentment bursts free with this new hope and new story.

This incident was a panacea for the Trump-hating portion of our society. There was a convergence between their need for a lead story, preferably an anti-Trump one, and their lack of hope. They now had renewed hope that the Trump presidency would finally come to an end. This convergence combines with the pent-up emotions from all the previous disappointments to provide the storyline and logic chain great energy and enthusiasm.

1. Trump is bad and dangerous
2. Trump is minimizing the dangers of COVID, endangering us all.
3. Minimizing COVID is bad and dangerous.
4. We must expose how minimizing COVID is bad and dangerous by exposing how bad COVID is.

When Fauci says that line, "ten times more lethal than the flu," he lit the fuse on the FEAR-19 Pandemic.

They had Trump now. All their dreams would be fulfilled.

Except, it was all based on lies, damn lies, and fake stats. Let me show you.

Lies, Damn Lies, and Fake Statistics

I believe that Dr. Fauci set off the "FEAR-19" pandemic when he used the line that COVID-19 was "ten times more lethal than the flu."

The storyline of how lethal COVID was, and how Trump was ignoring the experts, endangering us all, was embraced with enthusiasm by the Trump-hating portions of our population and the media.

But it was all built upon lies, damn lies, and fake statistics. Here we go…

We will start with Dr. Tedros, who made the statement:

"Globally, about 3.4% of the reported COVID-19 cases have died. By comparison, seasonal flu generally kills far fewer than 1% of those infected."

I saw that statement and immediately yelled, "that's not true; he's making a false comparison. Why is he exaggerating?" I was amazed. Why on earth was the WHO's Director-General giving misleading fake stats about the lethality of COVID versus the flu?

To explain why these are fake stats, we will go back to Dr. Fauci. The day after he lit the fuse on the "FEAR-19" pandemic, Dr. Fauci testifies in a hearing with the House Oversight and Reform Committee. His testimony repeats most of what he said to Hannity on FOX. His comments will help me show why the comparison Dr. Tedros made was misinformation and fake stats.

"For a practical understanding for the American People, the seasonal flu that we deal with every year has a mortality of 0.1%. The stated mortality overall of this (COVID), when you look at all the data, including China, it is about 3%. At first, it started out at 2, and now 3."

Now, Fauci knows this is a false comparison, so he walks it back a bit by saying:

"I think when you count all the cases of **minimally symptomatic or asymptomatic**, that probably brings the mortality down to somewhere about 1%."

Okay, there it is. Fauci explains that the second number is missing some things. You have to count the minimally symptomatic and asymptomatic.

In Tedros' comparison, one number he uses is the death rate for total infections of the flu, and the other is the death rate for confirmed cases of COVID. These two numbers are not even close to the same thing. The WHO Director-General made a false comparison that completely exaggerated the dangers.

It is a false comparison because he compares apples (confirmed cases) to oranges (total infections). It is a fake stat, and he knew it, just like Fauci did.

- Apples – Confirmed cases (only a part of total infections)
- Oranges – Total Infections

As Mark Twain said, "there are lies, damn lies, and statistics."

Comparing confirmed case mortality to the total infections mortality is not just bad statistics; it is a damn lie. Tedros knew that these were wholly different and uncomparable stats, just like Fauci did. It was a damn lie. The WHO Director-General was intentionally misleading the world with this fake statistic.

When Trump told Hannity he believed that number was false; he was 100% correct.

At one point during the early stages of this crisis, I remember telling my wife, "the most surreal thing is that Trump is the only one making sense." I guess I have a couple of points in telling you that. One, I am not a Trumper. Two, something was amiss; why is Trump making more sense than the "experts." And three, somehow, this non-Trumper became so upset that he decides to write a book criticizing Trump's opponents. UGH! How does this happen? Well, you are about to find out.

Okay, so the big question is, why would the Director-General of the WHO use fake stats? Easy, because this was about politics, not health.

Admittedly, I was naïve. I thought that the WHO was about health. Unfortunately, that is not always true. I was amazed when I saw Tedros make that comparison. I could not comprehend why he was flat out misleading people. So, I started looking closer, and what I found did not make me feel any better.

You see, Dr. Tedros and WHO have a history of making political moves to counter Trump. Let me show you a few things I found that will help clarify their motivations.

Remember when Trump issued the China travel ban back on January 29th of 2020? That ban goes into effect a couple of days later on February 2nd.

The very next day, February 3rd, the WHO holds its Executive Board meeting. During his presentation to the board, Dr. Tedros announces the new WHO recommendations to **"prevent and limit the further spread of the virus (COVID)."**

The number one recommendation to prevent and limit the further spread of the virus was, and I quote Dr. Tedros here:

"There is no reason for unnecessary measures that interfere with international travel and trade."

Wait; what? The WHO's number one recommendation to **"prevent and limit"** the spread of coronavirus is **not** to limit international travel. Seriously?

Think about that, does that even make sense? Even if they think travel restrictions are not needed, that's your number **one** recommendation? The WHO believes that is the **most important** thing we need to do, or should I say not do? Yeah, probably had nothing to do with Trump or politics. Watching that meeting was another epiphany moment for me, and not in a good way.

Here is a sampling of headlines the day after Tedros' statement on February 3.

- February 4, ABC News:
  "WHO Urges against China travel ban as coronavirus cases reach 20,000."
- February 4, Politico:
  "Coronavirus Quaranteen, Travel Ban could backfire, experts fear."

Trump issues ban, WHO's Tedros immediately stresses that limiting travel is bad. This announcement is like blood in the water for the press. I wish I could say that all Tedros was doing was giving credibility to criticisms of Trump, but he does not just do this for the media. Unfortunately, there is more to the story.

The following is a snapshot from the Newsmax article titled:**"China furious with US over growing travel ban."**

> Chinese government officials are angry with the United States over its growing travel ban in the wake of the growing coronavirus outbreak, pointing out that the World Health Organization has said stringent restrictions are not necessary.
>
> "A certain country has turned a blind eye to WHO recommendations and imposed sweeping travel restrictions against China," Hua Chunying, the Chinese Foreign Ministry's spokesman, tweeted on Saturday, reports **The Washington Post**. "This kind of overreaction could only make things even worse. It's not the right way to deal with the pandemic."

This article was published on the morning of Tedros' comments. China was obviously very unhappy about the ban, so a repudiation of Trump made them very happy.

But wait, how about another example of the WHO countering Trump?

Remember Trump calling COVID the Chinavirus?

The press reaction is predictable. Trump is a racist. Trump is a xenophobe, etc.

Then, in a WHO press conference on February 28th, a China Central Television reporter asks a question about "the origin of the virus." Before asking his question, the reporter **states** that scientists "are having no clear evidence the virus is from China."

Wait; what?

He then asks a pair of questions.

1. "Do you know the origin?"
2. "Does it mean came from China just because first case from there?"

Umm, well, okay, I guess that could be in question.

Dr. Maria Van Kerkhove fields the question instead of Tedros. She gives a long answer about animals and what they don't know about the virus but summarizes with; "**we do not have a clear answer yet.**"

Then, Dr. Michael Ryan jumps in and states, "**it is very important we don't ascribe blame on geographic origin.**"

- Trump issues China ban
  WHO #1 Recommendation to stop the spread of COVID is bans are bad.
- Trump calls COVID the Chinavirus
  WHO stresses not ascribing blame on geographic origin.
- Trump compares COVID to flu
  WHO uses fake stats to show COVID is way worse.

Yeah, the WHO is not concerned with Trump or siding politically with China at all.

I am no longer naïve about what is important to the WHO. That worries me for the future as a person scared of pandemics. The WHO is willing to give misleading information, including fake facts, for political reasons. Now, who do we trust?

At least we can trust our authorities, right?. Well, back to Dr. Fauci.

Here is that section of his testimony to the House we looked at previously.

"For a practical understanding of the American People, the seasonal flu that we deal with every year has a mortality of 0.1%. The stated mortality overall for this (COVID), when you look at all the data, including China, it is about 3%. At first, it started out at 2, and now 3. I think when you count all the cases of minimally symptomatic or asymptomatic, that probably brings the mortality down to **somewhere about 1%.** Which means it is **ten times more lethal than the seasonal flu**. I think that is something people can get their arms around and understand."

Look, I appreciate him pointing out the false comparison of the fake stats that became rampant in the media, but I have to take him to task. You see, he lied.

Fauci says it (COVID) is: "somewhere about 1%." He doesn't believe that.

He says, "10 times more lethal than the flu." He certainly does not believe it is ten times more lethal than the flu. He does not think the numbers he gives are accurate.

Are you asking, "how do you know what he believes?" "How do you what he thinks?" Good, I like skepticism. Let me show you how I know what he thought. I know he did not believe the mortality rate was 1%, and COVID was 10% more lethal than the flu because he told us. Well, not us.

———

You see, Dr. Fauci authored an editorial in the New England Journal of Medicine (NEJM) published on February 28th, **ten days before** his famous testimony in the House. Here is a quick snapshot from that report he wrote along with Dr. Robert Redfield, who also serves on the Coronavirus Task Force.

> patients had a wide spectrum of disease severity. If one
> assumes that the number of asymptomatic or minimally
> symptomatic cases is several times as high as the
> number of reported cases, the case fatality rate may be considerably less than 1%. This suggests that the
> overall clinical consequences of Covid-19 may ultimately be more akin to those of a severe seasonal
> influenza (which has a case fatality rate of approximately 0.1%) or a pandemic influenza (similar to
> those in 1957 and 1968) rather than a disease similar to SARS or MERS, which have had case fatality
> rates of 9 to 10% and 36%, respectively.[2]

To medical professionals, he writes, "COVID-19 may ultimate be more **akin** to a severe seasonal influenza." Not ten times worse but **akin**.

His **worst-case scenario** is that COVID is **similar** to the bad flu years in 1957 and 1968.

That is what he tells the medical professionals. But to the politicians, press, and the American public, he exaggerates so they can "get their arms around" it. What the hell? We deserve better. Just give people the science. Just tell the damn truth.

Okay, so maybe you are thinking, "but a lot changed in ten days."

Well, not so much. You see, on March 9th, MdRxiv published a report titled "Estimating the infection and case fatality rate of COVID-19 using age-adjusted data from the outbreak on the Diamond Princess cruise ship." Using that data, they determined that the real case mortality rate for COVID-19 in China was 0.5%. The **REAL mortality rate was 0.5%**, which is akin to Fauci's worst-case scenario.

Do you believe that Dr. Fauci was not up to date on all the science and all the most recent information? This study was released two days **before** his appearance in the House, and it confirms what Fauci wrote in his report was correct. Do you think he ignored information that proved he was correct?

Now, I have not even gotten to the most frustrating part. Remember how Trump was "not listening" to the experts? Remember how he was "ignoring the science"?

Fauci's report in the NEJM was published two days **after** Trump made the "you treat it like the flu" comment, and the same day Trump made the hoax comment. Two of three authors of the report, Fauci and Redfield, are on the task force advising Trump. This report is the **exact** information that Fauci and Redfield were giving to Trump. The "experts" were telling Trump that is was **akin** to the flu.

Trump was repeating precisely what his experts were telling him.

Now, let's connect a couple more dots to confirm that what Fauci was telling Trump is different than what he told us. Remember when Trump said, "you treat it like the flu"? If you go and watch the press conference on February 26th, both Fauci and Redfield were standing there with Trump. When you get to point where Trump says, "you treat it like the flu," he stops, looks over to Dr. Fauci, and says, "right Doctor?" To which Fauci says, "exactly."

Absolutely unbelievable! What the hell happened Fauci?

This discrepancy puzzled me initially. Why was Fauci saying two different things? Then, I watched his testimony to the House committee on youtube, instead of just reading it. He stresses the part when he says, "**10% more lethal than the seasonal flu.**" I think he was trying to scare people because he wanted us to take COVID seriously. It's a shame that his trying to give a "**practical**" understanding that "**people can get their arms around and understand**" did not begin with the truth.

I am a firm believer in the people. If given the truth, they can be depended upon to meet any national crisis. The great point is to bring them real facts.
Abraham Lincoln

Both Tedros and Fauci lied. Whatever their motivations were, political or altruistic, they both lied, and they both knew they were lying. Instead of an informed public, we started with lies, damn lies, and fake stats.

That line, "**10% more lethal than the seasonal flu,**" was the headline all over the place, and Fauci didn't even believe it. I think that Dr. Fauci's testimony was the moment the FEAR-19 Pandemic began.

The media, with its desire for a big story and its zeal to get Trump, accepted these lies, damn lies, and fake stats because they served their purposes. This fake information fits perfectly into their logic chain and gave them the path forward to remove Trump.

The truth, COVID was never more lethal than the flu, but if you tell a big lie and repeat it often enough, people will come to believe it. I will show you how the press grabbed hold and ran with the lies, damn lies, and fake stats without performing their due diligence to seek out the truth.

They didn't need to; they already **knew** the truth. "Through and through, balls to bone."

The COVID boogie man

March 10 was the beginning of what I am calling "The FEAR-19 Pandemic." Fauci's appearance on Hannity lit the fuse of a campaign that developed and cultivated fear, hysteria, and panic. Let's review the incidents leading up to that fateful event.

- February 26 – Trump, "you treat it like the flu" at a press conference.
- February 28 – Trump, "their new hoax," and again compares COVID to flu at a campaign event.
- February 29 – Trump again compares COVID to flu at First Coronavirus Task Force press conference.
- March 3 – Dr. Tedros uses fake stats to compare COVID and flu
- March 5 – Trump calls that number "false" on Hannity
- March 9 – Trump tweets comparison of flu and COVID
- March 10 – Fauci says COVID is "ten times more lethal than the flu" on Hannity's show.

We discussed the emotional state of the Trump-hating segment of our population, the democratic politicians, and the disproportionate number of the mainstream media.

- The need for a new lead story in the news, with the end of the democratic primary.
- The desperate need for some hope of getting rid of Trump.
- Bubbling vat of anger, frustration, and resentment due to repeated disappointing conclusions to their attempts to get rid of Trump.

We also discussed the beliefs of this group regarding Trump that they **know**, "through and through, balls to bone."

- Trump is a bad and dangerous man.
- Trump does bad things that endanger everyone.
- Because of this, we need to remove Donald Trump from office.
- Until Donald Trump's removal, we should resist or oppose him at all times, so he cannot do as many bad and dangerous things.

Those beliefs would continue to contribute to different logic chains. The following is the logic chain at the end of Fauci's comments.

1. Trump is bad and dangerous.
2. Trump is minimizing the dangers of COVID by comparing it to the flu.
3. Minimizing the dangers of COVID is bad and dangerous.
4. We must expose the real dangers of COVID to prove how bad and dangerous Trump is.

The lies, damn lies, and fake stats of Dr. Tedros and Dr. Fauci gave legitimacy to this entire chain of thought. This information was accepted without challenge because it reinforced their beliefs. Trump was ignoring and defying the experts and putting people in danger. **Now even Trump's supporters had to accept the truth**. He was FINALLY, FINALLY exposed for the bad and dangerous man he was. And, now we can FINALLY, FINALLY get him out of the White House. Hope was restored, and that pent-up energy was released.

It becomes one giant enthusiastic charge to expose how terrible COVID is and, by extension, prove how bad and dangerous Trump is to everyone.

Look, in saying this, I do not think this was intentional. The media probably did not know it was all false, but in their zeal, they forgot about their responsibility to investigate. Remember the article about the fourth estate titled, "The Fourth Estate- On the role of journalism. **Facts vs. Fake News.**" Here is another snapshot from that article.

This is were the press steps in. The press provides a vital role in discerning fact from fiction and reporting thereof from a neutral, unbiased perspective.

We assume expertise and a professional attitude on the part of the journalists, the providers of our news. This assumption implies something that is of even more value than expertise and professionalism: TRUST.

Trust is what binds us together, connects all the individual bubbles we call our reality. We rely on the press to record, investigate, interpret and publish the facts truthfully. We have to be able to trust our journalists. If they fail, we fail.

In their zeal to get Trump, they accepted fake facts without investigation, verification, and due diligence.

This book is not a defense of Donald Trump. I do not like the man and certainly do not believe he did everything right, but the *FEAR Pandemic* was a media and political creation. They are the ones that created the fear out of their desire to get Trump. They forgot to investigate and confirm. They did not discern fact from fiction. They failed, and in doing so, they violated the public trust.

The purpose of this book is to inform, so maybe that can be corrected in the future. We need some source of information that can be trusted.

Now, watch as I show you how they failed and became the **primary distributors of fake news over facts**.

On March 11, NPR releases an article titled "**COVID-19, How it Compares to other Diseases in Five Charts**." Here is their chart with the same apples to oranges fake stats comparing how deadly the flu is to COVID.

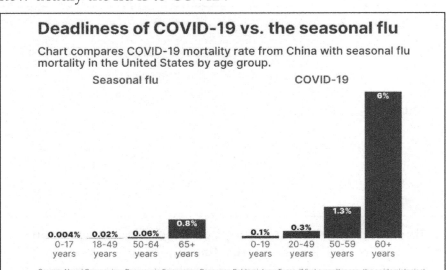

On March 13, VOX releases the story **"COVID-19 is not the flu, it's worse,"** along with their pretty chart full of fake stats.

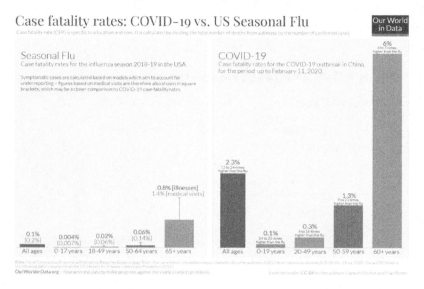

ABC News got into the fake stats chart game with **"COVID-19 had been compared to the flu. Experts say that is wrong."**

	More common in children	Some have body aches, nasal congestion, and diarrhea.
HOSPITALIZATION RATE	1-2%	10-20%
MORTALITY RATE	0.1-0.2%	1.5% (US). 4.5% (Global) *** numbers are estimates and likely to change.
HIGHEST RISK POPULATIONS	Children <5 yrs; older adults; chronic conditions (lung disease, heart disease,	Older adults; nursing home; chronic conditions (e.g. lung disease, heart

Business insider did their part supporting the storyline with their article on "**The coronavirus death rate in the US is far higher than that of the flu – here's how the 2 compare across age ranges**." They also include a helpful chart full of fake stats.

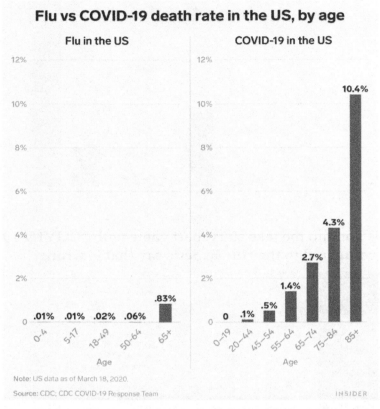

Flu vs COVID-19 death rate in the US, by age

Note: US data as of March 18, 2020.

Source: CDC; CDC COVID-19 Response Team

INSIDER

Lies, damn lies, and fake statistics. They were creating a COVID boogie man that was way worse than the real COVID.

These are just a few examples of charts that provide an excellent visual representation of how the media presented these fake stats. The stories about how bad COVID was, how it was much worse than the flu, flooded the internet, newspapers, and the talking heads on television for weeks after March 10th. It was everywhere.

But it was not just the promotion of fake news that created fear of COVID. It was also the other part of that original logic chain.

1. Trump is bad and dangerous.
2. Trump is minimizing COVID, so minimizing COVID is bad and dangerous.
3. We must expose how minimizing COVID is bad and dangerous.

During one press conference in March, Peter Alexander from NBC asks Trump, "**is it possible that your instinct to put a positive spin on things is giving Americans a false sense of hope?**"

At another press conference, Jim Acosta from CNN asked Trump, "**What do you say to Americans who are upset with you about how you downplayed this crisis?**"

And plenty of stories were published.

CNN: "**Trump peddles unsubstantiated hope in Dark Times.**"

Washington Post: "**Trump is spreading false hope for a virus cure, and that's not the only damage.**"

MSNBC: "**Trump gave Republicans false hope about coronavirus.**"

The press was fighting Trump's hope with fear. If they could create more fear, than they would expose that Trump's hope was dangerous. The drive to prove how COVID was terrible, and we all needed to be afraid was insatiable.

Here is a snapshot from the Yahoo article titled: **"Trump's overconfidence has always been dangerous. With coronavirus, it's deadly."**

This article provides a good look at the theme. Look again at the title and then read the excerpt.

> Good preparation and effective action are based on truth, not lies, however comforting. Officials do not reduce the risk of tragedy when they maintain, optimistically, that an impending disaster won't be so bad.

Truly unreal, right? "Preparation should be based upon truth!"

I could not agree more. We should have been preparing with the truth, but instead, we were preparing with lies, damn lies, and fake statistics for a mythical COVID boogie man that was a creation of the media. And this boogie man was the worst thing ever.

"Officials do not reduce the risk of tragedy when they maintain, optimistically, that an impending disaster won't be so bad."

Trump's optimism in the face of their boogie man was dangerous.

Look, these examples are just the tip of the iceberg. The COVID boogie man was the end of the world as we know it and must be feared. If you did not fully acknowledge the truth of how dangerous this boogie man was, you were not just dangerous, you were deadly.

And it was not just Trump being attacked for being honest, optimistic, or hopeful. Anyone who challenged the narrative on social media was attacked, bullied, or shamed. You were dangerous. You were trying to kill people. You were a bad person. They hyped up their boogie man and attacked anyone who challenged the narrative.

Doctors were pulled off Youtube for having a different opinion and challenging the false narrative. Here is Youtube's response to the news station that published the doctors.

"We quickly remove flagged content that violate our Community Guidelines, including content that explicitly disputes the efficacy of local healthy authority recommended guidance on social distancing that may lead others to act against that guidance," said the statement. "However, content that provides sufficient educational, documentary, scientific or artistic (EDSA) context is allowed -- for example, news coverage of this interview with additional context. From the very beginning of the pandemic, we've had clear policies against COVID-19 misinformation and are committed to continue providing timely and helpful information at this critical time."

These doctors were providing "**misinformation**" and had to be removed. However, to this day they still allow all the fake charts and fake videos full of misinformation.

How in the world have we gotten to a point where fake news is the only acceptable truth, and everything else is dangerous?

The media created a mythical COVID boogie man that was the most terrible creature ever. Then, they defended their boogie man against all evildoers.

The Brainwashing

When Fauci lit the fuse on the FEAR-19 Pandemic, the Trump-hating green journalists exploded. All the pent-up anger, resentment, and disappointment was released with the new hope of removing Trump and the gift of a new lead story. The race to expose how bad COVID is, and thus how bad Trump is, was on.

1. Trump is bad and dangerous.
2. Trump is minimizing the dangers of COVID by comparing it to the flu.
3. Minimizing the dangers of COVID is bad and dangerous.
4. **We must expose the real dangers of COVID to prove how bad and dangerous Trump is.**

Not only did they exaggerate the danger at hand with lies, damn lies, and fake stats, they used tricks.

Perception is more important than reality.

The first trick was connecting COVID to death. There were constant updates about COVID, this many confirmed **cases** and that many **deaths**. And the numbers would always be presented with a very exaggerated and descriptive adjective like dramatic, staggering, stark, or alarming. They were pounding into us the connection between getting infected and dying, prompting our subconscious to connect and equate the two things.

Confirmed **cases** and **deaths**. Total **cases** and total **deaths**. New **cases** and new **deaths**.

COVID=DEATH was hammered into our subconscious, creating fear.

In his book *Iconoclast*, Neuroscientist Gregory Burns describes perception this way:

"Perception is the brain's way of interpreting ambiguous visual signals in the **most likely explanation** possible."

To further build the COVID=DEATH connection, they would use this trick of perception. They would use visuals along with their commentary to also connect the two perceptually.

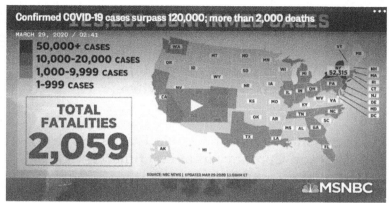

We continuously see COVID and DEATH together, so our minds would connect the two as the **most likely explanation**.

Additionally, they would regularly use the color red in the charts, either for the text or in the background. This use of red is also a little psychological trick. Red is a color that stimulates the brain. It also represents danger. Below is a WHO visual to show what I mean. I realize this next chart is in black and white for the book, but all the little circles of infection were in red. Danger! Danger!

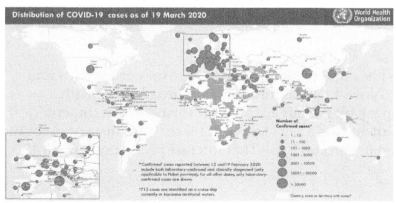

They were not just exaggerating the severity of COVID; they were using perceptual and psychological tricks cultivating fear, hysteria, and panic about its lethality.

COVID=DEATH

Red Alert, Red Alert.

COVID=DEATH

Over and over, they were brainwashing us. They were creating perception, not informing. Every time you would turn on the computer, your phone, everywhere,

COVID=DEATH

I want you to see a snapshot from Google Trends search results for COVID and Coronavirus at that time. The chart shows the amount of interest for a particular word.

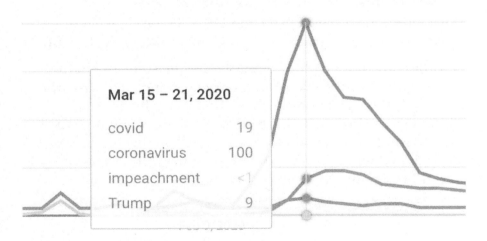

Mar 15 – 21, 2020	
covid	19
coronavirus	100
impeachment	<1
Trump	9

The two lines that peak on the right are for coronavirus and COVID. Now, to put it into context, the two lines with a smaller peak on the left are for Trump and impeachment. Impeachment was a big story, but there was a historic amount of interest in coronavirus. That interest peaked on March 15th – March 21st.

This level of interest was a panacea for the Trump-hating green journalists. They had more attention than ever because people were desperate for information.

Instead of responsibly informing people, they exploited that desperation to continue their campaign of exposing how bad COVID was to prove how bad Trump was.

1. Trump is bad and dangerous.
2. Trump is minimizing the dangers of COVID by comparing it to the flu.
3. Minimizing the dangers of COVID is bad and dangerous.
4. **We must expose the real dangers of COVID to prove how bad and dangerous Trump is.**

They were building and cultivating their COVID boogie man instead of informing the public.

The more people watched, the more fearful they became.

The more fearful people became, the more they watched.

The more people watched, the more fearful the became.

They just kept the snowball rolling downhill.

The fear, the hysteria, and the panic were all increasing at a scary pace. The boogie man was becoming more and more powerful. And they just knew their boogie man was going to punish Trump.

But the boogie man was built on lies, damn lies, and fake stats.

Real Mortality Rate

Now that you understand how they created their COVID boogie man, let me show the truth about what COVID is, and always has been. Not their mythical COVID boogie man but the true COVID.

There are two types of tests for COVID. The first test is for the virus; it checks to see if you are currently infected.

The second type of test is for antibodies. If you catch COVID and recover, your body will develop antibodies. If you have antibodies, that means you were previously infected. Your body developed the antibodies fighting the infection.

New York has done a large amount of antibody testing. They tested random samples of the population to see how many people had been infected by COVID and now have antibodies.

They discovered that 21.2% of the population of New York City had antibodies as of April 23rd. This result means that 21.2% of the population had been infected with COVID and recovered.

The population of New York City is approximately 8,551,000 people, so COVID had infected approximately 1,800,000 people (21%) in New York City.

At the time of the testing, there were 147,000 confirmed cases of COVID and 10,290 COVID deaths.

1. 1,800,000 total COVID infections in New York City
2. 147,000 confirmed cases of COVID in New York City
3. 10,290 deaths in New York City
4. 0.57% case mortality rate for COVID in New York City

Wait; what? 0.57% mortality for COVID? That is not what we have been told.

No, it is not. But it is correct, at least at that time.

The actual infection mortality rate of people infected with COVID in New York City as of April 23rd is 0.57%, according to the study results.

Let's compare that to the mortality rate being given by the media at that time.

- COVID Confirmed case mortality in New York City: **7.0%** (used by media)
- COVID total infection case mortality in New York City: **0.57%**

Lies, damn lies, and fake statistics.

We were continually fed a meaningless stat because it fed the fear, and it all began with Dr. Tedros' original damn lie and fake statistic.

Let me take you back to his comparison. Understanding how big an exaggeration that was is the key to understanding how this all happened.

Remember, he is explaining to the world the differences between COVID and the flu.

"Globally, about **3.4% of the reported COVID-19 cases have died**. By comparison, seasonal flu generally kills far **fewer than 1% of those infected**."

Now look at the difference between the two statistics (confirmed cases and total infections) in New York City that I just showed you.

7.0% for confirmed cases and 0.57% for infections.

I have said Tedros was comparing apples and oranges. I think a better analogy would be that he was comparing a tire to a car.

The tire (confirmed cases) is only a small portion of the car (total infections).

New York City numbers.

- Confirmed cases – 147,000
- Total Infections – 1,800,000

The confirmed cases are only 8% of the total infections. Saying those two numbers are comparable is inaccurate, and Dr. Tedros knows this. Dr. Tedros flat out lied and offered fake stats.

The Director-General of the World Health Organization intentionally misled the world about the severity of COVID because of politics.

Is that scary for you? It damn sure is to me.

The media accepted the fake stats without confirmation because "getting Trump" and having a big story was more important than verifying information. Green journalism at its worst.

---

green journalism

This term is a criticism of modern **journalism**. It references to "**yellow journalism**" - a term used for the sensationalistic journalism during **the turn** of the 20th century. The green refers to money and the greed of the industry and/or the pro-environmental bias.

*Often as sensationalistic as its yellow predecessor, green journalism tends to appeal to our emotions, exploit our fears, and **pander** to our vanity. It places a political agenda in front of **the quest** for journalistic truth and in its most demagogic forms tolerates no criticism, branding all who question it as enemies of the people.*
*-Jack **Shafer***

That is the definition of green journalism from the urban dictionary. I could not have said it better myself. Let me give you an example of a well-known journalist putting his political agenda ahead of journalistic truth.

On March 9, MSNBC had an expert on the *11th Hour* show with Brian Williams. The guest was a disease specialist and epidemiologist, Dr. Celine Grouper. You know, an expert on this stuff. Brian Williams said to Dr. Grouper, "please explain, for the record and our audience the **danger of comparing this to influenza**."

In her answer, she states, "we are looking probably at a case fatality rate, best case scenario, **at the 0.5%,** which is still several-fold higher than the **traditional flu**."

The expert epidemiologist just revealed that the Director-General of the WHO exaggerated this number with fake stats. **Why didn't Williams follow up on that?**

Because he did not care, look at his "question." He did not ask whether COVID and the flu were comparable. He **directed** her to explain why the comparison was dangerous.

Brian Williams had no interest in the truth of Dr. Tedros using fake stats. He had no interest in the truth that Trump was right when he said they were false numbers. He was not even interested in whether or not COVID compared to the flu. Those truths were irrelevant. All Brian Williams wanted to do was support his false belief, his bias, and his logic chain:

1. Trump is bad and dangerous.
2. Trump is minimizing COVID by comparing it to the flu.
3. Comparing COVID to the flu is bad and dangerous.
4. We must expose that comparing COVID to flu is dangerous to prove that Trump is bad and dangerous

For Brian Williams, the Doctor stated COVID was several-fold worse than the flu, perfect. Mission accomplished.

Except, that is not what she said.

What Dr. Grouper states is, "still several-fold higher than the **traditional** flu."

Why did she say "traditional" flu? Why not just say flu? Because that would be a lie, and the good doctor was at least trying to be honest, even if she didn't give us the whole truth.

You see, there are good and bad years of the flu. 0.5% would be a bad year of the flu. So, she uses the word "traditional."

Let's talk about this "traditional" flu. Most people do use the number of 0.1% to express the infection mortality rate of the flu. That is the same number used by Fauci, and I have no reason to disagree with that representation. That is a fair number for an average, or "traditional" year of the flu.

But, there are good and bad years of the flu. The worst recently was 2017-2018, which had a mortality rate of 0.13%.

Remember, in Fauci's report in the New England Journal of Health, when he mentioned the 1957 and the 1968 pandemic years? Those were bad years for the flu.

The 1957 flu had a mortality rate of 0.67% and saw 1.5 to 2 million deaths worldwide.

The 1968 flu had a mortality rate of 0.5% and saw 1 million people die from the flu worldwide.

And of course, there was the flu in 1918. That is estimated to have had a mortality rate of 10-20% and killed 50-100 million people worldwide.

The recent testing in New York City indicated a 0.57% mortality rate for COVID. Let's compare that to those other years.

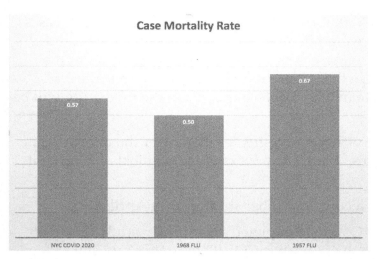

Case Mortality Rate

NYC COVID 2020	1968 FLU	1957 FLU
0.57	0.50	0.67

COVID has always been like the flu. **Maybe, maybe** a bad year of the flu, but akin to the flu.

We also talked about the report from MdrXiv that was published the same day as the good doctor's appearance on MSNBC. That report identified the real mortality rate at 0.5% in China. I would suspect that the good doctor read that report to prepare for her interview. That was the science at the time, not the exaggerated numbers coming from Dr. Tedros and the media.

Now, I think the final mortality rate will end up being considerably lower than 0.5%. Remember in my opening when I explained that the mortality number **always** comes down. That was why the reported 2.3% mortality rate from China was good news to me; I knew it would end up way lower. And that is already happening.

Let's go back to the Diamond Princess Cruise ship. On May 6, The Centre for Mathematical Modeling of Infectious Disease, CMMID Repository, released a study that investigated the testing results from the same Diamond Princess cruise ship.

They reported that more than half of the asymptomatic cases were undiscovered by the timing and type of testing used. The asymptomatic cases were closer to 75%, instead of the almost 50% on the initial reports. Because of this, the 0.5% mortality rate in China determined from the first study will be even lower.

The more the science investigates, the lower the rate will go. It always does. I don't know exactly why; I just know that it does.

Let's look at a couple of other studies from April.

Los Angeles County completed an antibody study on April 8th. Their results indicate a COVID mortality rate of 0.18% in Los Angeles County.

Interesting, right? That rate is still higher than the "traditional" flu's 0.1%, but much closer to 0.13% in 2018, just two years ago. And that is way lower than a bad year of the flu.

Another antibody test performed by Stanford medical in Santa Clara County, California, was completed on April 1. Those results indicate a 0.06% mortality rate for COVID-19 cases there. This report identified the upper limit of COVID-19 mortality at 0.2%. The **upper** limit.

On the higher side, if you look at the numbers from all of New York instead of just New York City, you get 0.76%. These numbers will be all over the place because the effects of COVID will vary from location to location and sample size. But, it is easy to see that the mortality rate is considerably lower than what is still being reported.

Why isn't this being talked about everywhere? Isn't this all good news? Because...

1. Trump is minimizing COVID
2. Minimizing COVID is bad and dangerous.
3. Studies minimizing COVID must be bad and dangerous.
4. We must expose studies minimizing COVID as bad and dangerous.

Here is a headline from Psychology Today: "**Does Stanford owe us an apology for that COVID-19 Study?**"

Alexander Danvers, Ph.D., a doctor of **Social Psychology**, is the author. Here is his opening paragraph.

> A team of researchers from Stanford recently posted a preprint of a manuscript on COVID-19 cases that was wrong. Based on their results, they suggested that many more people had already had the virus than we realized. The upshot was supposed to be that maybe it didn't cause symptoms as often as we thought, or that maybe we'd get to "herd immunity" more quickly and less painfully than we thought.

The Social Psychologist Dr. Danvers asserts that Stanford researchers were wrong and are falsely claiming that "(COVID) didn't cause symptoms as often as we thought."

How dare they claim that COVID is less severe than we said? The study was obviously wrong according to the Social Psychologist. He **knows** it is wrong.

I won't bore you with his reasoning in the article, but his conclusion is:

"**research coming out of Stanford and published on top scientific journals is more likely to be speculative and razzle dazzle than research from middle tier institutions and middle tier journals**."

You know what, I can understand that. I am a skeptic myself and completely believe you will get more razzle-dazzle than truth from the mainstream media, so maybe it's that way in research as well.

Let's test the Stanford results to see if they owe us an apology. We can check those results against three other antibody tests that came out in April. There's was the first but there were three more after that.

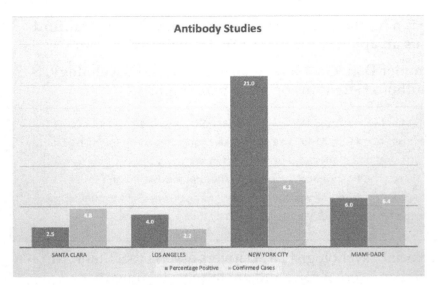

All four tests showed that confirmed cases were well under 10% of total cases. New York City was the highest at 8.2%. That means the other studies confirmed Dr. Danvers's fears. **More people are asymptomatic then they thought**. Stanford was correct. We will discuss all of this in more detail in the next chapter.

The point right now is that this study exposed a weakness in the COVID=DEATH mantra, so it **had to be exposed as bad and dangerous.**

Thus, **Stanford needs to apologize** because they did not tow the party line and prove how bad COVID is.

I ask again, how did we get to the point that fake news is the only acceptable truth?

COVID vs FLU

Here is a snapshot of the testing protocols for New York as of May 14.

Protocol for Testing

As New York State aggressively expands COVID-19 diagnostic testing capacity, the Department of Health has revised guidance to increase testing for frontline workers, including all first responders, health care workers, and essential employees who interact with the public, while continuing to prioritize resources. Testing for COVID-19 shall be authorized by a health care provider for individuals who meet one or more of the following criteria:

- An individual is symptomatic or has a history of symptoms of COVID-19 (e.g. fever, cough, and/or trouble breathing), particularly if the individual is 70 years of age or older, the individual has a compromised immune system, or the individual has an underlying health condition; or
- An individual has had close (i.e. within six feet) or proximate contact with a person known to be positive with COVID-19; or
- An individual is subject to a precautionary or mandatory quarantine; or
- An individual is employed as a health care worker, first responder, or other essential worker who directly interacts with the public while working; or
- An individual presents with a case where the facts and circumstances — as determined by the treating clinician in consultation with state or local department of health officials — warrant testing.

If you have symptoms, you get tested for the COVID virus. If you do not have symptoms, you do not get tested for the virus.

If you are infected but do not have symptoms, you are an asymptomatic case. I prefer to use the term "not sick." You can be infected with COVID and still be "not sick."

As we discussed, the antibody study in New York City indicated that there were approximately 1,800,000 COVID infections, but only 147,000 confirmed cases. The other 1,653,000 estimated cases were asymptomatic or minimally asymptomatic. They were not sick or not sick enough to think anything about it and go to the doctor.

That means 92% of the people infected by COVID in New York City were "not sick."

So, the study indicates the most likely result for anyone infected by COVID is they will be "not sick."

Did you catch that?

The **most likely result** for anyone infected by COVID is that they will be "**not sick**."

That is excellent news, right? Maybe someone should talk about that and let people know.

Virulence is a measure of the severity of a virus on its host.

> Virus virulence can be measured in a variety of ways, based on mortality, illness, or pathological lesions, each of which can be quantified. The virulence phenotype also may be qualitative, involving differences in the tropism of different viral variants. Wild-

We can compare virulence by measuring deaths or amount of illness. So far, we have focused on the infection mortality rate, but you can also compare the amount of illness.

The asymptomatic rate for the flu is 75%. We can compare that to the results from the antibody studies we discussed.

Asymptomatic

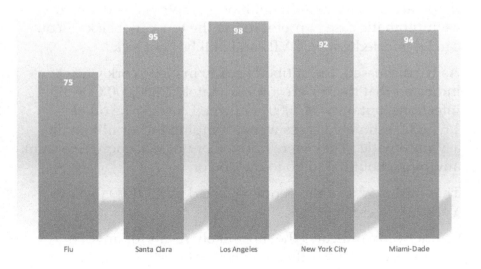

This data reveals COVID may be less severe, less virulent than the flu because there is a lower incidence of illness. That is why Dr. Danvers was upset about the Stanford study; it revealed a possible weakness in their COVID boogie man.

There is a lot of data to come in and be evaluated; we need to ensure that those cases were asymptomatic and not something else. But this is another reason why I believe the mortality rate will continue to drop as they learn more.

One of the significant differences between COVID and the flu is how they compare across age groups. Let's use numbers from the CDC to compare the percentage of deaths from the flu and COVID by age group. We can compare those numbers to the percentage of the overall population and see which age groups are underrepresented and overrepresented. These results will allow us to gain some insight into how the virulence shifts across age groups.

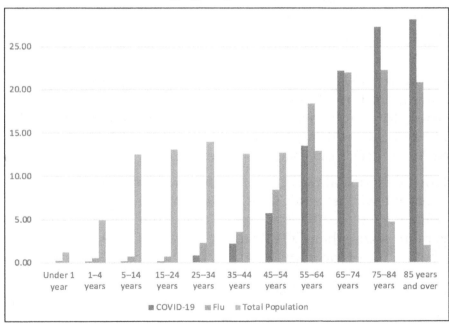

There are several interesting things you get from this data. First, the severity of both viruses increases dramatically with age. Both viruses are incredibly damaging to the elderly. COVID is much more destructive than the flu to everyone who is 65 or over.

COVID is scary lethal to the elderly, especially those with underlying conditions.

91.1% of all deaths from COVID are from the 65 and older groups. And they only represent 26.95% of the population. 83.6% of flu deaths are from this same age group. This age group is significantly overrepresented with both viruses. Both of these viruses are devastating to this age group, but COVID is clearly the worst.

Now, the numbers look even dimmer if you move up to 75 years of age and older. This group has 55.4% of the deaths and only represents 6.7% of the population. You have got to be kidding me, that is not good. Yea, the flu is rough as well, with 43.15% of the deaths. But COVID is making a direct assault on our elderly.

My father is 81 years old, has diabetes, blood pressure issues, a family history of heart problems, and even some history of respiratory problems. My father has a target on his back. We are doing everything we can to keep this thing away from him. COVID is devastating to the elderly.

However, look at the differences for everyone else. For everyone who is under 65, there is a considerably higher percentage of deaths from the flu than from COVID. The flu is more severe than COVID to everyone younger than 65. That is 73% of the population.

Let's take a closer look at the lower age groups.

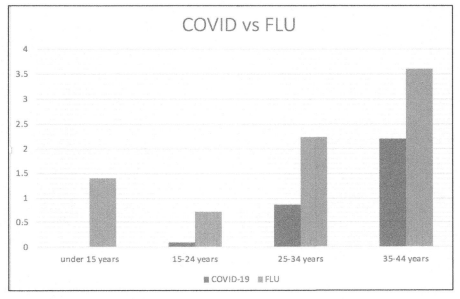

While the flu bounces back in virulence with the very young, COVID just disappears. This detail is one of the significant differences between COVID and the flu, and it is one of COVID's weaknesses.

It's not that COVID is akin to the flu. That is only true statistically across the age groups in total. In the different age groups, the comparison changes.

COVID is more severe than the flu for anyone 65 and older.

Flu is more severe than COVID for anyone under 65.

And to the young, the flu is significantly more severe. COVID does very little damage to the young.

Spain did an excellent job of tracking infections, hospitalizations, ICU stays, and deaths across all age groups. Let me show you those results.

It is disappointing that our CDC cannot be better at this. They use different age group categories for each stat. So comparisons are not possible. But let's look at the data from Spain.

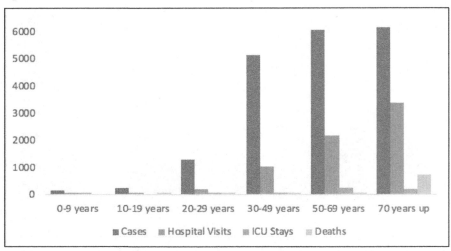

The younger you are, the less severe the illness will be. Not just death, you will be significantly less sick, if sick at all. There are fewer ICU stays, hospital visits, and confirmed cases as you get younger. The one thing this chart does not list is asymptomatic cases (not sick). But they will follow the same pattern.

There will be significantly more deaths at the older age groups, and there will be substantially more asymptomatic infections at the younger age groups.

"But they can still catch the virus."

Yes, I know, of course they can. The contagiousness of a virus has nothing to do with age. Contagiousness is a characteristic of the virus, not it's intended host. Droplets of water containing the virus do not differentiate between the age of the intended host. So, exposure to the virus will be pretty consistent across age groups.

Using that correct statement of "they can still catch it," we can make some statistical estimates regarding asymptomatic symptoms across the age groups. So, back to data from Spain.

We will begin by saying there are no asymptomatic infections in the over 70 age group. There will be, but we want our estimates in the younger groups to be conservative.

Assuming that exposure and infection will be consistent across the age groups, we can estimate the number of "not sick" for each age group. This chart represents the percentage of not sick and deaths per age group in Spain.

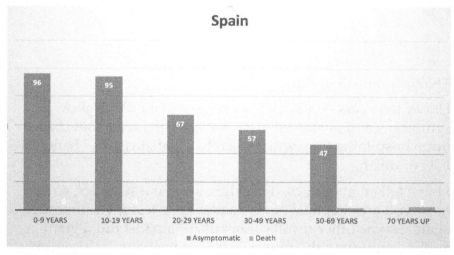

This data indicates that 95% of everyone under the age of twenty who get infected with COVID will be asymptomatic.

Let's look even closer at the younger age groups and include other COVID severity measures. We can put the confirmed cases, hospitalizations, and ICU data back into the chart.

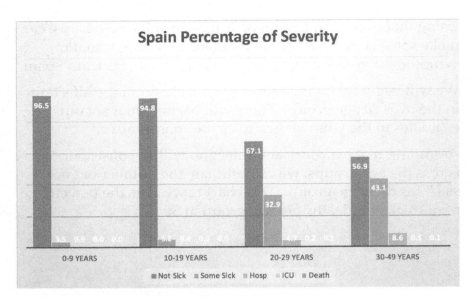

Spain Percentage of Severity

Legend: Not Sick, Some Sick, Hosp, ICU, Death

- 0-9 YEARS: 96.5, 3.5, 0.9, 0.0, 0.0
- 10-19 YEARS: 94.8, 5.2, 0.4, 0.0, 0.6
- 20-29 YEARS: 67.1, 32.9, 4.7, 0.2, 0.1
- 30-49 YEARS: 56.9, 43.1, 8.6, 0.5, 0.1

That is interesting, right?

Under ten years of age, 96.5% asymptomatic, 3.5% show symptoms and get tested, 0.9% have severe symptoms based upon hospitalization, with basically a statistical 0% chance of ICU or death.

I have talked about lies, damn lies, and fake statistics, so I hope you are skeptical of my math. Let's test my estimates against some other results. Luckily, Spain just did a giant antibody study with around 90,000 participants. This study presents an excellent opportunity to check my estimates. They did not break this study down by age groups, but we can still check the total to see if my calculations are in line.

On May 16, Spain reported that approximately 5% of the population had antibodies. That indicates that 2.34 million people were infected. If you subtract the confirmed cases (those sick enough to get tested), you would have 2.062 million potential asymptomatic COVID infections.

- 2.34 million people infected with COVID in Spain.
- 2.062 million asymptomatic (not sick) infections.

Now, if you go back to my estimates and add up all the asymptomatic from every age group, you get 2.21 million. I missed it by 150,000. Not spot on, but pretty close to the results from their actual antibody testing. The math is there; the theory is sound.

Everyone under twenty years of age has about 95% chance of being asymptomatic (not sick), less than 1% chance of severe illness, and an almost 0% chance of ICU or death.

Here is a snapshot from the *Medical Express* website about colds.

> The common cold is normally a mild illness that resolves without treatment in a few days. And because of its mild nature, most cases are self-diagnosed. However, infection with rhinovirus or one of the other viruses responsible for common cold symptoms can be serious in some people. Complications from a cold can cause serious illnesses and, yes, even death—particularly in people who have a weak immune system.

Doesn't that completely summarize the effects of COVID on younger people? With younger people, comparing COVID to the flu may be an exaggeration. COVID is probably more comparable to a cold to those under 20 years of age.

Understanding the true severity of COVID and the way it changes across age groups would be critical to developing a suitable containment and mitigation plan.

Instead, we used lies, damn lies, and fake stats to develop an utterly illogical and destructive plan based upon a mythical COVID boogie man.

Silent Carriers

Let's go back to the beginning of March and review the emotional state of the Trump-hating portion of our society.

- There was a cauldron full of anger, frustration, and resentment boiling over due to a string of emotional disappointments.
- There was also desperation for something to give them hope of finally removing Donald Trump from the presidency.
- And, there was a need for a new lead story within the media.

Trump had been minimizing COVID and comparing it to the flu. Along comes Fauci with his line "ten times more lethal than the flu."

The convergence between the emotional state and string of events led to an explosion of energy into the COVID storyline. They did not question any of the information because they just **knew** it was correct, "through and through, balls to bone."

The result was the development of a mythical COVID boogie man who was the most dangerous monster ever, and the boogie man was going to punish Trump. Keep in mind what was fueling their thinking at this point; they were going to prove that Trump was bad and dangerous by exposing how bad COVID truly was.

1. Trump is bad and dangerous.
2. Trump is minimizing the dangers of COVID
3. Minimizing the dangers of COVID is bad and dangerous.
4. **We must expose the real dangers of COVID to prove how bad and dangerous Trump is.**

All the anger, all the frustration, all the **disappointment** poured out, and that energy went into exposing how bad the boogie man was. Because of all the past disappointments, their collective psyche could not consider any possibility other than COVID is terrible, and Trump would finally be removed because he endangered us all.

I already gave you one example with the Stanford test, where the science was not just ignored but attacked because it didn't support their narrative. They labeled it lousy science and controversial. The only thing controversial was that it did not support the myth of the COVID boogie man.

Understanding this dynamic is essential to understanding what comes next because the next characteristic of the COVID boogie man would become the worst of them all. **What should have been good news was sold as the worst possible problem imaginable.**

In February, China reported that 80% of cases were minimally ill, and the early report from the cruise ship reported 50% asymptomatic. It was always known that there were a significant number of asymptomatic cases, so why didn't we hear more about those statistics.

Because of COVID=DEATH!

Things that make COVID seem less severe are bad.

Asymptomatic (not sick) people make COVID seem less severe.

1. Trump is bad and dangerous.
2. Trump is minimizing COVID.
3. Minimizing COVID is bad and dangerous.
4. The number of Asymptomatic people minimizes the dangers of COVID.
5. We must expose asymptomatic people as bad and dangerous.

Along comes the concept of the "silent carrier." That name is terrifying and sounds like it is right out of a horror movie. Perfect!

"Silent carriers" make COVID seem terrible, so that is AWESOME! Plus, it eliminates the discussion about people being "not sick" because those people are scary and dangerous.

This is the psychology at play and why the asymptomatic spread "**problem**" was embraced so enthusiastically.

Asymptomatic people are not the problem; they are the solution.

As Colonel Jessep said, "you can't handle the truth."

Their collective psyche could not handle another possible disappointment. The COVID boogie man had to be the worst thing ever, and so, the "silent spreaders" had to be the worst thing ever.

The "silent spreaders" were the perfect psychological protection. They were an unsolvable problem that would always keep the boogie man scary and powerful. That is why it was embraced so enthusiastically.

It was this dynamic that turned the solution into a problem. Again, **Asymptomatic people are not the problem; they are the solution**. I will show you why they are the solution shortly.

Now, let's make sure you understand the amount of potential asymptomatic (not sick) infections we are talking about.

We have discussed how the antibody studies began revealing a high number of asymptomatic infections, possibly as high as 90%. The full extent of asymptomatic illnesses is still not entirely known; there is more data to come in.

With the releases of more and more antibody studies, it is becoming apparent that the number of asymptomatic cases is significant. I will add a few more completed antibody studies from May to the chart I previously gave you.

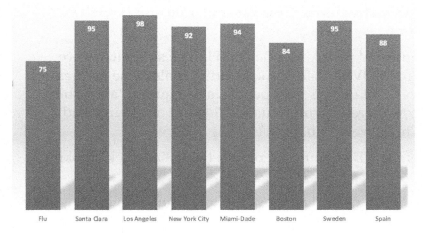

Asymptomatic

Flu	Santa Clara	Los Angeles	New York City	Miami-Dade	Boston	Sweden	Spain
75	95	98	92	94	84	95	88

If you get infected with COVID, the most likely result is that you will be "not sick."

If you are young and get infected with COVID, the **overwhelmingly** likely result is that you will be "not sick."

To me, the number of infected people who were not getting sick was excellent news.

The good news does not stop there. These studies were identifying people testing positive for antibodies. Your body develops antibodies when you become infected and then recover from the infection. The great thing about antibodies is that they afford you some level of immunity. More people having antibodies reduces the ability of the virus to spread.

Good news, right?

- A lot of infected people being "not sick" is good news that makes COVID seem less severe, so that gets ignored.
- People being immune reducing the ability of the virus to spread is also good news, so it gets ignored.
- Asymptomatic "silent spreaders" are scary and an impossible problem to solve, so that gets embraced.

Here is one of my favorite examples. Let me show you an article from CNN that shines a light on this thinking.

The story was titled: "**We need to fix it quickly. Asymptomatic coronavirus cases at a Boston homeless shelter raises red flag.**"

Four hundred people at a Boston Homeless Shelter were tested for COVID. 146 of those individuals came back as positive. Out of those 146 people, and I quote, "all of them were considered asymptomatic." 146 out of 146 infected individuals were "**not sick.**"

How is my 90% number of people being "not sick" looking now.

That is 36.5% of the homeless shelter population having some level of immunity after they recover. And keep in mind, they tested for the virus, not antibodies. It is likely that others within the shelter already had antibodies, increasing the overall immunity of the homeless population as a whole.

They never even considered that this was good news. They were **incapable of that thought; it had to be a problem**. To me, 146 infected homeless people without any symptoms of illness, who would soon be immune, is excellent news.

Now, the fascinating part of this is they needed to fix the problem of people not being sick and being immune. The insanity is unreal, the ultimate example of mass hysteria. This narrative was continually rammed down the throats of the American people in an attempt to cultivate that fear and hysteria.

> "These are larger numbers than we ever anticipated," said Dr. Jim O'Connell, president of the Boston Health Care for the Homeless Program. "Asymptomatic spread is something we've underestimated overall, and it's going to make a big difference."
>
> O'Connell said Thursday that across the country medical professionals have just been looking for signs and symptoms in homeless people. While Boston aggressively tested residents at a second shelter after the asymptomatic findings, the city is considering what to do next, he said.
>
> "All these things we are recommending for social distancing, you can't do that when you walk into a shelter," O'Connell said. "I think it is a real failure on our part, and we need to fix it quickly."

"Asymptomatic spread" is something they "underestimated overall." Well, no, actually, what you did was exaggerate the severity of the virus, making you underestimate the number of "not sick." I can see how that is a problem for you.

The original premise was that COVID is "ten times more lethal than the flu." Never was and never will be. But if you had invested a tremendous amount of effort into building this boogie man, totally believed how dangerous he was, and invested all your hopes that your boogie man would punish Trump, you may be psychologically incapable of just letting it go. "We need to fix it quickly."

So instead, this weakness of COVID became a terrible problem, dominating the narrative. Just more lies, damn lies, and fake statistics.

The asymptomatic have always been the solution, not a problem. But of course, solutions are bad because they weaken the COVID boogie man. Instead, let's create an unsolvable problem.

Here is another snapshot of the same article.

> O'Connell said that the local and state government is collaborating with the CDC about how to proceed. He said the collaboration between different partners is necessary because the "problem is with the dimension of this virus" -- and he noted that even with all of this help, they might not be able to tackle the problem.

State and local governments are collaborating with the CDC because of the difficulty of this "dimension" of the virus. Even with all this help, they may not be able to "tackle this problem."

They are all going to collaborate to tackle the problem of too many people not being sick and to many people becoming immune. I swear the whole thing is just becoming a group mental disorder. I may need to look closer at the Trump Derangement Syndrome; it is starting to make a lot more sense now.

I have no idea how they are going to tackle this problem.

If you get infected with COVID, the most likely outcome is that you will be "not sick."

If more people recover and have antibodies, the spread will slow.

That is terrible news. Whatever will we do to solve this problem?

We will come back to the issue of virus spread and discuss the solution, but for now, I just want you to see the psychology at play. The thought of people being "not sick" being good news does not even cross their minds.

I will give you one more example. Chelsea, Massachusetts, was a hotspot. They did antibody testing on a small sampling of residents in the middle of April. What they found is that 32% of the population had antibodies, versus 2% of the population being confirmed cases.

Chelsea has a population of 40,000 people, and 2% is 800 people. The study indicated that 32% were infected, which would be 12,800 people. That means that 12,000 COVID infected people were "not sick." Twelve thousand people had been infected but not sick enough to get tested. 12,800 people, 32% of the population, had antibodies giving them some level of immunity. Good news or bad news?

However, it was enough to confirm the fears of local authorities, who renewed calls for people to follow social distancing rules.

Twelve thousand people being "not sick," twelve thousand people having some level of immunity, **confirmed the fears of authorities.**

The high emotional investment into COVID being so terrible made it impossible to see even the possibility of any positives.

"You can't handle the truth." Their collective psyche could not handle another disappointment. The COVID boogie man had to be the worst thing ever.

In the beginning, we knew we could not stop the spread, so we were trying to flatten the curve to ensure the health system could handle it. But when COVID was starting to reveal itself to the masses as less severe than reports, suddenly we had to solve the unsolvable problem of stopping the spread.

It was the perfect pivot for those who were unable psychologically to accept that COVID was not the worst thing ever; they could embrace the horror of "silent carriers."

On some level, I feel bad for them because denial will only get you so far. Eventually, they will have to look at the truth, and that is going to be painful. I only hope there is a lesson to be learned before they just repeat the pattern. But I doubt it.

Their inability to even consider people being "not sick" and immune as a good thing led us down a path of destruction.

Asymptomatic people were never the problem; they have always been the solution. I will show you how shortly.

Chicken Little for President

The sky is falling. Life will never be the same again.

So far, I have only been focusing on the Trump-hating green journalists in the media. But there was another group that has played a significant role in the scam. This segment of society genuinely despises Trump, wants to bring him down and loves attention. Yes, the politicians in the Democratic party. The journalists and democrat politicians are perfect compatriots.

The politicians joined the battle to fight Trump by showing how bad COVID was. It was a total frenzy. It became a race to see who could get the most attention and who could attack and blame Trump the most.

Democratic Governors became the perfect Chicken Littles. They began running around, yelling how the sky was falling, and the world would never be the same again. They're telling us how Trump is trying to kill us all. The Chicken Littles are giving more fake stats, and the media would treat those stats like they were real. Twitter spats start popping up all over with the media promoting the "good guy" Governors who were trying to save us, and the "bad guy" Trump, who was letting people die or worse, trying to kill them.

And all of it was founded on lies, damn lies, and fake facts.

There are endless examples, so I am only going to highlight a few.

On March 18, Gov. Gavin Newsome sent a letter to Trump with their projections for California. Their forecasts predicted that 56% of the population of California would be infected within eight weeks. The Governor's office immediately released the letter to the press for promotion.

OFFICE OF THE GOVERNOR

March 18, 2020

The Honorable Donald J. Trump
White House
1600 Pennsylvania Avenue, NW
Washington, D.C.

Dear Mr. President,

I write to respectfully request you immediately deploy the USNS Mercy Hospital Ship to be stationed at the port of Los Angeles through September 1, 2020, to help decompress our current health care delivery system in Los Angeles region in response to the COVID-19 outbreak.

As you know, California has been disproportionately impacted by repatriation efforts over the last few months. Our state and health care delivery system are significantly impacted by the rapid increase in COVID-19 cases. In the last 24 hours, we had 126 new COVID-19 cases, a 21 percent increase. In some parts of our state, our case rate is doubling every four days. Moreover, we have community acquired transmission in 23 counties with an increase of 44 community acquired infections in 24 hours. We project that roughly 56 percent of our population—25.5 million people—will be infected with the virus over an eight week period.

This resource will help decompress the health care delivery system to allow the Los Angeles region to ensure that it has the ability to address critical acute care needs, such as heart attacks and strokes or vehicle accidents, in addition to the rapid rise in COVID-19 cases. The population density in the Los Angeles Region is similar to New York City, will be disproportionately impacted by the number of COVID-19 cases.

I would ask that the US Navy coordinate with my Office of Emergency Services, through the Defense Coordinator Officer to rapidly deploy this asset.

I thank you for your partnership and look forward to our continued discussion.

25.5 million infected people is an incredibly large and scary number, right? The fake mortality rate in the media at that time was around 5%. That must mean that 1.275 million Californians were going to die. Oh no, the sky is falling, we are all going to die! Lies, damn lies, and fake statistics.

Governor Witmer in Michigan got into her spat with Trump and was suddenly a Vice Presidential possibility. If you were a good enough Chicken Little and not afraid to call out Trump, you got rewarded with the spotlight.

We all remember Gov. Cuomo in New York. He would just go on and on about the ventilators that Trump would not send him.

NY Post: **"Coronavirus in NY: Cuomo defends need for 30K ventilators after Trump called it overblown."**

Cuomo is trying to save us, but Trump is just going to let New Yorkers die. I remember someone saying he was going to let people die because of politics. Here is a snapshot from that article.

> "All the predictions say you could have an apex needing 140,000 beds and about 40,000 ventilators," Cuomo said at a press briefing Friday at Manhattan's Javits Center. The state's predictions come from Weill Cornell Medicine, the CDC and the consulting firm McKinsey and Company.
>
> Cuomo, without mentioning Trump by name, added, "I don't have a crystal ball. Everybody's entitled to their own opinion, but I don't operate here on opinion. I operate on facts and on data and on numbers and on projections."

Damn, that is a lot of beds and a lot of ventilators. He is operating "on facts and on data and on numbers and on projections." Cuomo is a hero because he is working on facts, while Trump ignores science. What facts, Gov. Cuomo? Fake facts?

He continues.

> briefing
>
> "I hope some natural weather change happens overnight and kills the virus globally. That's what I hope, but that's my hope, that's my emotions, that's my thoughts. The numbers say you may need 30,000," Cuomo said.

See how the themes all run together. Cuomo could not be emotional; he had to stick to reality. And, Trump's misplaced hope would get people killed.

Cuomo was such a great Chicken Little that suddenly he was a presidential candidate.

Here is a snapshot from an article titled:

"Yes, Andrew Cuomo Can Be Nominated for President in 2020"

Larocca, a former State Transportation Commission, candidate for Governor himself, and current Village Trustee in the Suffolk County village of Sag Harbor, made a straightforward case for Cuomo, contrasting the New York governor's leadership against the utter failure of Donald Trump, and the lack of command of the crisis coming from either Joe Biden or Bernie Sanders:

"Contrast this with Cuomo's management of the coronavirus emergency in New York. He has been clear-headed and clear-voiced, and that has been comforting. As a result, New Yorkers and their families understand what they must do to survive. And the governor is out there managing the state's response, relentlessly foraging for critical medical supplies and equipment, and pushing the Trump administration and the federal bureaucracy to make better decisions.

Cuomo is the best Chicken Little, always at it with the sky is falling, and also excellent at going at Trump. This type of leadership is what is needed to lead the democratic party. You can't make this stuff up; it is so entertaining.

Now, Cuomo said he was operating on facts and numbers. Yea, lies, damn lies, and fake statistics. Let's see how that went.

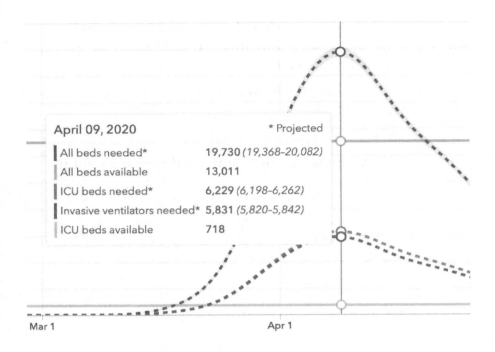

April 09, 2020	* Projected
All beds needed*	19,730 (19,368–20,082)
All beds available	13,011
ICU beds needed*	6,229 (6,198–6,262)
Invasive ventilators needed*	5,831 (5,820–5,842)
ICU beds available	718

Mar 1   Apr 1

According to the online resource *covid19.healthdata.org*, New York City peaked on April 9 at 19,730 beds and 6,229 ventilators.

That is a little less than the 140,000 beds and 40,000 ventilators Cuomo needed so desperately. Who exactly was operating on the facts and numbers Governor Cuomo? It seems your "overblown" need as Trump called it, was just more lies, damn lies, and fake statistics.

New York only ended up needing 15% of the ventilators they originally projected. **Only 15% of projections** in our most significant outbreak area. Where was the frontpage story sharing the good news??? Do I hear crickets?

Cuomo also had Trump send him the Navy hospital boat, they set up emergency hospitals at convention centers and colleges and sent out a call for help from medical health professionals from all over the country. They needed all of this because so many people were going to die. The sky was falling.

Here is a Reuters story only a couple weeks after he complained about the ventilators.

"New York City hospitals cancel temporary workers as coronavirus cases stabilize."

> But New York, which ramped up its hospital bed capacity to around 90,000, has had only about 18,000 patients hospitalized for the past several days.
>
> "We are seeing contracts in New York get cancelled," Lindsey Scott, a spokeswoman for staffing agency Trusted Health, said in an email. "The hospitals in New York hired a ton of travelers as the crisis started to ramp up, and then either had more nurses than they needed, or in some cases, more than they could ingest into the system."
>
> She said Trusted Health had "multiple nurses who left their families and in some cases full-time jobs," to travel to New York, only to find that they were no longer needed.
>
> Karla Guerra, 27, an emergency room nurse from Arizona, said her contract at New York's Mount Sinai hospital system was abruptly canceled on Monday, the day she completed her onsite orientation. She had expected to earn $32,000 for eight weeks' work.
>
> Now, she is $3,000 out of pocket for her travel and first month's rent, and is trying to find a new contract as soon as possible.

This pattern was repeated all over the country. Crazy amounts of money spent to set up emergency hospitals that were not needed because expectations were exaggerated. They were preparing for the COVID boogie man, not COVID.

The Chicken Little cries about the sky falling were all projections built upon a mythical COVID boogie man. Lies, damn lies, and fake statistics.

Let's do one more, Trump press conference on March 19, right in the middle of the fear-mongering and Trump-hating frenzy. In the press conference, Trump is optimistic about the drug hydroxychloroquine. And of course, it is suddenly the most dangerous and untested drug in the world. Trump is trying to kill people again.

At this point, the frenzy is almost comical. I mean, it was surreal. I think the Trump-hating crowd totally lost their minds. So, a couple of actual facts.

- Hydroxychloroquine approved for use in the US since 1955
- Doctors can prescribe approved drugs for off label use
- Hydroxychloroquine is on the WHO's Essential Drug List

Look, even the WHO thinks it is safe and effective, that's why it is on their Essential Drug List, and it has been used safely in the United States for 65 years.

But, "TRUMP IS TRYING TO KILL EVERYONE WITH HIS REFUSAL TO MAKE DECISIONS BASED UPON SCIENCE!"

Two Governors banned the use of Hydroxychloroquine for COVID patients. They used **their** medical expertise to tell the doctors how to treat their patients. Don't worry, they backtracked a few days later and called it all a miscommunication, nothing to see here.

There are still arguments going on about Hydroxychloroquine's safety and effectiveness because people are so invested in Trump being wrong.

The whole period was surreal. It was hard to believe what was going on. The attention-seeking and Trump-hating politicians were non-stop with their contributions to the lies, damn lies, and fake stats.

The media supported and promoted the Governors' fake information. But it was not just the politicians and the media. Twitter, Facebook, etc. were all ablaze with attacks on anything that minimized COVID or complimented Trump. The hostility was scary.

And it was all based upon lies, damn lies, and fake statistics. How did we get to the point that fake news is the only acceptable truth?

It would have been entertaining, except there were terrible consequences. You see, after building up the terrifying COVID boogie man, they had to contain and mitigate him. They were not trying to contain and mitigate COVID; they were planning to fight a mythical monster, and unfortunately, the damages caused fighting their mythical boogie man were real.

I have wondered what would have happened if Trump had said that COVID was the worst thing ever.

1. Trump is bad and dangerous.
2. Trump says COVID is terrible.
3. Exaggerating COVID is bad and dangerous
4. We must expose how COVID is not that bad to prove Trump is bad and dangerous.

They would have told us it was a harmless little kitty cat. I mean, remember the reaction at the beginning of February when Trump issues the travel ban. "Flu is a bigger threat," and "flu is deadlier."

Amazing!

The Lockdowns

Oh boy, here we go again.

On March 23rd, Donald Trump tweets, **"WE CANNOT LET THE CURE BE WORSE THAN THE PROBLEM ITSELF."**

He follows that up on March 24th with, **"I would love to have the country opened up and raring to go by Easter."**

And they are off. Trump is still defying the experts and putting us all in danger.

I'll just pull one headline from CNN:

"Trump says he wants country 'opened up and just raring to go by Easter' despite health expert's warnings."

1. Trump is bad and dangerous.
2. Trump wants things open.
3. Things being open is bad and dangerous.
4. We must expose that things being open is bad and dangerous to prove that Trump is bad and dangerous.

Suddenly the Trump-hating people, including the media and politicians, embraced the lockdowns with all their hearts and souls.

Trump wants things to open up, so hunker down folks, we will need to remain locked up forever.

Suddenly, things were getting canceled in June, then July, then closed for the summer, maybe next fall. Sports would never look the same again. School? Nope. Canceled. We weren't sure what the next two weeks would look like, but we needed to cancel Christmas. There were even cries that we would not be able to come out until there was a vaccine. Life will never be the same again!. This is our new normal!.

Thanks for letting me know the sky is falling, Chicken Little.

All of these concepts fit together quite comfortably with the mythical COVID boogie man the Trump-haters had created.

- COVID is the worst thing ever; it is more severe, more lethal, more dangerous than anything we have ever experienced.
- The asymptomatic cases are the biggest problem because they are "silent spreaders."
- We have to stay locked down indefinitely to stop these "silent spreaders" from killing everyone due to how bad COVID is.

And anyone who disagreed with any of this was bad and dangerous. The online attacks on anyone who questioned anything became intense. Let the shame games begin. People were shamed, verbally attacked, and in some cases, had their material pulled from the platforms.

The pressure on politicians everywhere to not only lockdown but to extend the lockdowns was immense.

And it was all based upon lies, damn lies, and fake statistics and fueled by a hatred for Trump.

Sweden is one of the few countries that did not put a lockdown in place. They resisted the pressure to fight the **mythical COVID boogie man** by shutting down the country and controlling every aspect of life. Instead, they came up with a plan for the **actual COVID** that would cause minimal disruption to life while trying to protect those most vulnerable to this virus.

Sweden banned events over 50 people, they closed museums, canceled sporting events, and they prohibited visits to nursing homes. But basically, that was it.

The borders stayed open, schools stayed open, there were no limits on public transportation or outings to parks, restaurants and bars could keep serving, hairdressers, gyms, and even cinemas remained open.

Sweden took a good bit of bad press, as you can imagine.

1. Trump wants things open.

---

2. Being open is bad and dangerous.
3. Sweden is bad and dangerous because they are open.
4. **We must expose that Sweden being open is bad and dangerous to prove Trump is wrong.**

Now, Sweden completed an antibody study on its population. The results indicated that 7% of the population had antibodies. This result was lower than their scientists had projected before the testing.

Here is a snapshot from an article in Business Insider. You remember Business Insider; they were one of the fake chart crowd, so they are very representative of the COVID boogie man team. They are in that "**we must expose that Sweden being open is bad**" section of the media.

The title of their article: "**A new Swedish coronavirus antibody study suggests the herd-immunity strategy isn't working.**"

> A new study suggested that only a small percentage of people in Sweden's capital, Stockholm, had developed coronavirus antibodies, casting doubt over whether the country's avoidance of strict lockdown measures is helping the population develop a significant level of immunity.

Success. They had exposed that Sweden failed because they did not lockdown.

I think I get it, Sweden's plan of no lockdowns failed because not enough people got infected. Wait, I don't get it. Is that good news or bad news?

You can't make this stuff up. I am officially on board with the Trump Derangement Syndrome concept. Talk about blinded by hate; they cannot even see the irony. They call Sweden's plan to stay open a failure because they had a **lower than expected rate of infection**.

So, would Sweden have been considered successful if they had more infections?

Are they arguing Sweden should have locked down to increase infections?

On March 24th, Trump stated that he would like to see the country open up by Easter. Suddenly, a large portion of the country and the world believed lockdowns were the only solution to stop the spread, and if anyone disagreed, they were dangerous and putting lives at risk.

Let's talk about the need for these lockdowns.

The lockdowns were a containment strategy against the **mythical** COVID boogie man based upon these two concepts.

1. COVID is highly severe and lethal.
2. The "silent spreaders" were dangerous because COVID is highly severe and lethal.

Both of these statements are wrong. COVID was never as severe and lethal as they wanted it to be to a majority of the population.

The second statement only exists because of the first, although it is also wrong. Asymptomatic people are the solution, not the problem. We will come back to that.

Because of the zeal to fight, resist, expose, and destroy Trump, we ended up in entirely unnecessary and ineffective lockdowns. The lockdowns have already had devastating consequences, and we have no idea what the long-term effects are going to look like. I am not even talking about the economic repercussions here. Everyone agrees there are going to be massive and long-lasting economic consequences from the lockdowns.

But that isn't even the proper discussion because the economic consequences are just the beginning. The argument that this is a question of lives over money is simply specious nonsense meant to distract us from the real cost.

- Trump is bad and dangerous.
- Trump cares more about making money than saving lives.
- Lockdowns save lives, and lives are more important than money.

Blah, blah, blah. It is a specious argument because it feels good superficially, but it ignores the true costs. I am so glad you can feel good about yourself and shame others because of your bullshit argument. How about we look at the real-life costs of the lockdowns?

Do you remember how COVID severity reduces significantly with age?

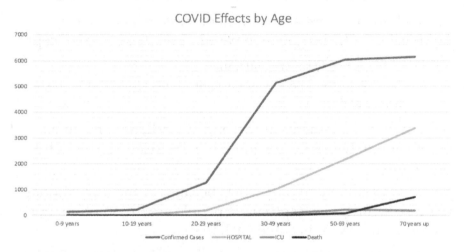

COVID Effects by Age

As of May 16th, there are 12 deaths from COVID in the USA from children under the age of 15. That is 1 death for every 5 million children.

I am literally getting angry writing this because I know where this is going.

Stanford Children's Health estimates that 2000 children under the age of 15 die each year from **accidents in the home**. Children are 166 times more likely to die in a home accident than COVID. We locked them up in their homes, which are **166 times more dangerous to them then COVID**.

But that little stat is just for perspective on how little risk children are at from COVID.

This is where I want to cry; it upsets me so much.

The following snapshot is from the American Psychological Association.

Risks for children

Children are also especially vulnerable to abuse during the pandemic, says child psychologist Yo Jackson, PhD, associate director of the Child Maltreatment Solutions Network at Penn State. Research shows that increased stress levels among parents is often a major predictor of physical abuse and neglect of children, she says.

And the resources many at-risk parents rely on — extended family, child care and schools, religious groups and other community organizations — are no longer available in many areas. Many child-protective organizations are experiencing strain with fewer workers available, so they may be unable to conduct home visits in areas with stay-at-home orders. While such operational changes may lead to inaccurate reporting of child abuse and neglect, Jackson says she and her colleagues are expecting a surge in abuse cases all over the country.

"Even parents who have great child management skills and great bonds with their kids are going to be tested," says Jackson. "There's a perfect storm happening in millions of homes for kids to be at greater risk for these negative interactions. "

We were so damn busy arguing how children are the "silent carriers" that are going to kill their grandparents that we forgot our duty to protect one of our most vulnerable populations, our children. How many children were locked away in bad situations only made worse by the stress? And with no supports? How come that is not all over the damn press?

I love how the article points out that even parents with solid skills will be tested while being locked down with their children. Remember all the jokes on Facebook about parents having to deal with their kids?

Think about homes where there are already severe challenges because of issues with the parents, the children, or both. Now magnify that by locking them together 24/7 with no supports in place. How do you think that went?

1,720 children die each year from abuse or neglect, 143 times more than have died from COVID, according to the report from *childwelfare.gov*. Do you think that number decreased with 24 hours a day, seven days a week containment? Do you figure everything went well?

Add in no social interaction, the inability to get respite and just take a break, or get help, and no opportunity for someone to intervene, provide supports, or notice the effects of abuse and report it was all gone.

And 1,720 is just the number of deaths. How many other children will suffer from a lifetime of trauma due to what happens to them during this time? My day job is working with troubled young children, many of whom suffered from horrible abuse, so I have witnessed its effects. There are **real costs** to the lockdown beyond the economic ones.

If you argued this debate was a tradeoff between lives and money, you should be embarrassed. If you ever made the argument that children are dangerous instead of vulnerable, you are complicit in the adverse effects suffered by those decisions. **It was "selfish" to expose one of our most vulnerable populations for your political and emotional gain.**

Children were never at risk from COVID, but they were selfishly put at risk because we could not take an honest look at the information. We knew they were not at risk from COVID before any school shut down. We knew they were not at risk from COVID before any shelter in place was issued.

Children were not at risk from COVID, but we put them at risk from a variety of much worse things. And now we are keeping them at risk over bullshit politics and our emotional needs. Absolutely disgusting!

And this is just one issue; there are the health effects of people locked in their homes for extended periods of time, drug and alcohol issues, the mental health needs that developed, were exasperated, or underserved, the child hunger issues, the impact of social isolation on children, and on, and on, and on.

This article was from the Washington Post on May 4th.

The coronavirus pandemic is pushing America into a mental health crisis

Anxiety and depression are rising. The U.S. is ill-prepared, with some clinics already on the brink of collapse.

I will leave you with one more. This report is from ABC7 news on May 21st.

"Suicides on the rise amid stay at home order, Bay area medical officials say."

The numbers are unprecedented, he said.

"We've never seen numbers like this, in such a short period of time," he said. "I mean we've seen a year's worth of suicide attempts in the last four weeks."

Kacey Hansen has worked as a trauma nurse at John Muir Medical Center in Walnut Creek for almost 33 years. She is worried because not only are they seeing more suicide attempts, she says they are not able to save as many patients as usual.

RELATED: Get help with mental health issues

"What I have seen recently, I have never seen before," Hansen said. "I have never seen so much intentional injury."

The trauma team is speaking out because they want the community to be aware, for people to reach out and support each other and for those who are suffering to know they can get help.

But yeah, this is all about lives being more valuable than money. If you made this false argument to avoid discussing the real dangers of lockdown, you should be ashamed. The lockdowns did not save lives; it just traded them. The lockdowns did not slow the spread of COVID; at best, they only delayed the spread. The lockdowns were an attempt to fight a mythical monster that had devastating consequences.

If you are one of the people who just accepted everything you were told as gospel, I hope these last few pages were an epiphany. This moment is your chance to decide if you are going to continue drinking the "kool-aid" moving forward, or if you will challenge false narratives.

Lies, damn lies, and fake statistics combined with a zeal to get Trump to create horrifying consequences.

———

Lockdown Failure

It is May 26, 2020, and I am finishing the book today. There is an awakening coming. We are getting closer to the time when they can no longer hide the facts or spin the story enough to validate their decisions, and I want to be on the record before that happens.

The lockdowns were ineffective, period, end of sentence. Well, except for saying period, end of sentence.

The lockdowns are the result of fighting a mythical COVID boogie man instead of coming up with solutions for COVID. They were ineffective and counterproductive for dealing with the real COVID.

There will be a lot of better information in the months ahead that will prove my point about being ineffective. The long term will be the most telling. Coming out of lockdown will cause spikes and extend the length of infection spread. Instead of letting the virus run its course, we have kept it around for a more extended period of time. Genius!

I am going to share some data that currently exists. Please continue to follow the data and share the results.

I am going to show you a few statistics from May 26th. Take them with a grain of salt as they only tell part of the story, and you should always be skeptical of statistics. That is why Mark Twain said, "lies, damn lies, and statistics."

I will not cherry-pick specific stats to make my point; I don't need to. You do have to cherry-pick stats to prove that the lockdowns accomplished anything, which is my point. If it's not obvious that it worked, was it worth it?

We talked about Sweden and how they did not lockdown. As of today, they have one of the highest daily deaths per million people in the world. Wait, before you start yelling, *see, they needed to lock down*, let me continue.

The country they are battling with for that distinction is Great Britain. Great Britain did have a significant lockdown. I am going to show you their graphs of daily deaths from *Our World in Data*. I am also including the United States.

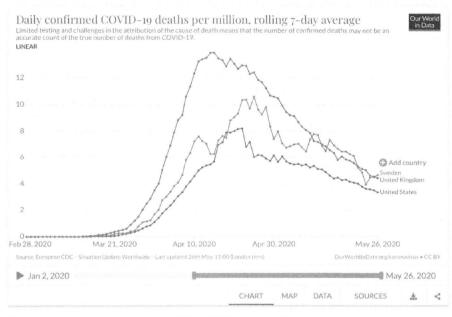

Do you see any remarkable differences?

We could include other countries into the chart as well, like their neighbor Norway and argue Sweden did terribly. Or, we could show a chart that includes Italy and Spain to demonstrate Sweden did great. But those arguments would be nuanced at best. Certainly not definitive, just like this one.

There are arguments and points on both sides about which approach was better. And that is my point; there is no clear evidence that either method was more effective than the other at limiting COVID deaths. Which means, there is no clear evidence that the lockdowns accomplished anything.

Let's look at a few better examples from the United States.

In the United States, six states did not impose a mandatory lockdown. The best possible comparison to show the results are states that border each other and have similar population densities. They share geographic location, demographic makeup, population size, and population density. Pretty much the best comparisons I can think to show you. There are three of these comparisons available.

We can visualize the differences between locking down and not locking down. This data is also from May 26th. I will use confirmed cases/daily cases charts and daily death charts side by side for you to compare. These charts are from *coronavirusbellcurve.com.*

Arkansas (no lockdown) and Mississippi (lockdown)

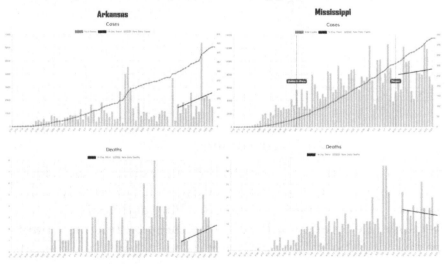

Look at the rising lines for total cases and see if you see any difference in how fast the virus spread. The total cases went on almost identical paths.

Nebraska (no lockdown) and Kansas (lockdown)

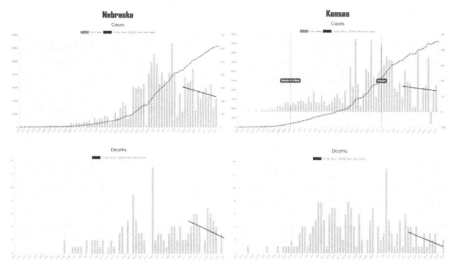

Differences? Or nearly identical?

Wyoming (no lockdown) and Idaho (lockdown)

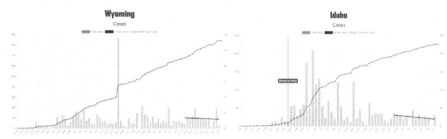

If someone wants to argue about the differences in the neighboring states and why this is all somehow worse than it looks, have at it. But if I removed the labels and you just had the charts, you would not be able to identify the lockdown state from the non-lockdown state. And these states have similar geographic, demographic, total populations, and population density.

When you consider the cost to individuals, families, businesses, and the economy, you would think there would be a tremendous amount of indisputable evidence of how the lockdowns helped save lives. However, the only proof that the lockdowns were effective or saved any lives is purely anecdotal storytelling and philosophy.

The lockdowns happened because of an emotional need to fight against the "bad orange man," not because they were needed, or would decrease the number of deaths. The Trump-hating crowd with their green journalists caused a pandemic of fear that has created far more devastating consequences than COVID ever could have by itself.

There is no honest scientific debate. There is just a need to hold on and resist Trump. To hell with the cost.

I am done with this discussion. Let's move forward.

The Way Forward

The contagiousness of a virus is pretty much constant. Its ability to spread from host to host is a characteristic of the virus. One of the problems with COVID-19 is that it is highly contagious. It is exponentially more contagious than the flu.

There are two ways to reduce the virus's ability to spread through the population.

- Containment measures
- Increased group immunity

We implemented several containment measures, everything from social distancing up to lockdowns. These containment measures work to limit the spread of the virus.

Another thing that can reduce the spread is group immunity. The more people within the group who are immune, the harder it is for the virus to spread.

Antibodies provide immunity. Antibodies are developed by our immune system when battling the virus. Those antibodies then give some level of protection against the virus. How much immunity, and how long it lasts, is not precisely known, there is a lot more research to do. But there is some immunity.

COVID-19 was a novel (new) coronavirus. It was free to spread through the population because no one had any antibodies to fight it. I said it WAS novel because it will never be new again. Therefore, it will never be as dangerous as it was.

That is what happens with the bell curve. A novel virus is free to spread at first, but once people develop immunity, the spread reduces. The more people who become immune, the less the virus can spread.

There are two ways to develop antibodies and immunity, you can get a vaccine, or you can recover from infection. There will not be a vaccine for some time, so that was never the solution. So, to increase immunity, we need people to become infected and recover.

The only way through is through; containment measures can slow the spread, but in the end, the virus has to run its course.

That is why there was the "flatten the curve" concept. We were never going to stop the spread; COVID was always going to cause significant deaths. But we could take measures to make sure there were not any additional deaths due to the system being overwhelmed.

Then, politics got involved. We went from flattening the curve to stopping the spread.

Trying to stop the spread is counterproductive because the only way to stop the spread is to have spread. People have to become infected and recover by developing antibodies.

Spread is not a problem. You want infection spread; you just don't want death.

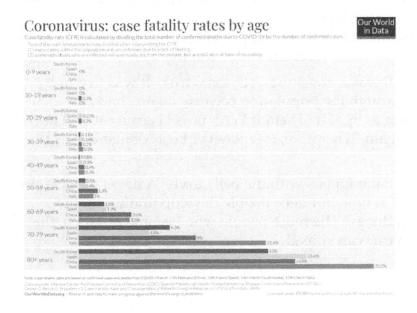

Stunning, right? That is data from four of the early outbreaks. COVID's severity is similar to the flu overall, but there is one massive difference between COVID and the flu. COVID is devastating on our elderly and almost harmless to our young.

You never attack an opponent's strength; you exploit your opponent's weakness.

Lockdowns were an attempt to fight COVID's strength, its contagiousness. We need to exploit COVID's weakness, its low severity against younger individuals.

How Vaccines Work

Vaccines help develop immunity by imitating an infection. This type of infection, however, almost never causes illness, but it does cause the immune system to produce T-lymphocytes and antibodies. Sometimes, after getting a vaccine, the imitation infection can cause minor symptoms, such as fever. Such minor symptoms are normal and should be expected as the body builds immunity.

Once the imitation infection goes away, the body is left with a supply of "memory" T-lymphocytes, as well as B-lymphocytes that will remember how to fight that disease in the future. However, it typically takes a few weeks for the body to produce T-lymphocytes and B-lymphocytes after vaccination. Therefore, it is possible that a person infected with a disease just before or just after vaccination could develop symptoms and get a disease, because the vaccine has not had enough time to provide protection.

That is from the CDC website explaining how vaccines work. The vaccine gives you a little bit of the virus, so your body develops antibodies, increasing your immunity. Did you notice the CDC mentioned that there was a chance of minor symptoms from the vaccine? Does this remind you of COVID's effects on younger people? A small risk of minor illness.

The young are not the dangerous "silent carriers" that are going to kill our elderly population. They are the shield. We have a large percentage of people that can develop antibodies with minimal risk, just like getting a vaccine. It's like a big societal COVID vaccination.

Our asymptomatic youth are not dangerous and selfish, "silent carriers." Our youth should not be afraid of COVID; it should be afraid of them. If they get infected and develop antibodies, we increase our group immunity, thus protecting our elderly. The only selfish act would be hiding away, avoiding a virus they can help defeat.

Our youth are our strong warriors who can take the fight to COVID. They are our shield and I, for one, plan to join them in that battle without fear. I am not going to try to get the virus, but I refuse to be afraid. And if I get it and survive (which is extremely likely), I know we will be that much closer to protecting people like my father (who have a high chance of death if infected).

The only way through is through; you have to want a solution to find one. COVID's primary weakness is that it does not impact younger people. We can exploit this weakness to take away its strength, its contagiousness.

There are four different age categories for COVID severity.

- Group 1: Under 20 years of age
  - Almost 0 chance of death
  - Low chance of illness
  - Severity comparable to a cold
- Group 2: 20-40 years
  - Minimal risk of death with an underlying condition, healthy practically 0 risk
  - Minimal illness
  - Less severe than the flu
- Group 3: 40-64 years
  - Some risk of death (especially with underlying conditions)
  - Some illness, comparable severity to flu
- Group 4: 65 and up
  - Very high risk of death (magnified with underlying conditions)
  - Strong chance of illness
  - More severe than the flu

Limiting spread or containing spread is not a black and white issue. That is reductive. We need to look at where we do and do not want to limit spread.

We do not want to limit infection spread in group one. I am not saying have chicken pox parties, but I am saying that we are not concerned about exposure to this group. If they get infected, fine, and, if they show symptoms, we will keep them home, just like we do with colds, the flu, or any other illness.

Group two is pretty similar to group one; however, anyone with underlying conditions needs to be careful, just like before COVID. Otherwise, get out there and do your thing.

Now, we get to group three. This group is the toss-up and a little harder to interpret. The most significant factor is your health. The stronger your immune system, the safer you are. We do not want to ignore spread with this age group, but we do not need to take severe measures. You would need to develop individualized containment plans depending upon the situation.

We want to contain all spread to this age group if possible. We do not want anyone in this age group to get infected if possible.

The solution has never been that complicated. We want COVID to spread to those it will hurt the least, and we do not want it to spread to those it will hurt the most. The more asymptomatic infections, the better. People being asymptomatic is not the problem; it is the solution. And it always has been.

It is not selfish to go outside and risk infection. It is selfish to hide inside, avoiding infection when your risk of severe symptoms is low. You can develop antibodies that will help keep the spread from those who are at higher risk.

We can defeat COVID. Here are the steps.

Step 1: We stop saying that "asymptomatic" people are a problem. They are the solution. This step requires a paradigm shift for a particular segment of the population.

Step 1A: We stop trying to contain spread to everyone and focus on containing spread to group four and anyone else with underlying conditions.

Okay, that's it. That's the whole plan, or at least the objectives.

Yes, there are a million logistical issues. Think of all the effort that went into the impossible task of stopping COVID from spreading to everyone. If we put half that energy into this plan, it would be achievable, and there would be a lot less collateral damage.

Think about it. If we invested our energies into keeping the virus away from our elderly instead of wasting time trying to protect those who are at minimal risk, we would limit deaths.

We are a great country full of a lot of smart people, and we can sort this out. As long as we can let go of political motivations and decide we want to solve the problem. The real problem is not COVID; it is politics.

I will spitball a few ideas to get it started.

We call things COVID ON or COVID OFF. COVID ON means that we are practicing social distancing, wearing masks, and all the other steps necessary. COVID OFF is life as usual. It's not that complicated.

Stores can have COVID ON hours and COVID OFF hours. For example, a grocery store can be COVID ON from 7-9 with a thorough cleaning at the beginning of the COVID ON period. The rest of the day could be COVID OFF.

Restaurants can be COVID OFF as long as they provide curbside pickup or delivery within a certain distance to anyone who is COVID ON.

Parks can COVID OFF and maybe COVID ON a specific day of the week. Or, some parks are COVID ON all the time.

Schools and colleges can open as usual with supports and conditions for those who are at-risk. We can come up with plans for those who have disabilities, why can't we come up with a plan for people at-risk from COVID.

Resorts could be COVID OFF or, maybe they have special COVID ON areas with different procedures.

The golf course could have COVID ON days and COVID OFF days.

Hotels could be COVID ON in the lobby and then have COVID ON floors. They can take breakfast to the people at higher risk and allow others to get breakfast.

We come up with plans for COVID ON and COVID OFF everywhere.

And then people figure it out based upon their situation.

For example, my house is a COVID OFF home. But my parent's house is a COVID ON house. Everyone should avoid going into my parent's house, and my parents should avoid going into any of the COVID OFF houses.

If you are a family with two parents in the early 30s and three kids, all healthy, have at it. Go to whatever COVID OFF thing you want. But don't visit the grandparents, for now, just skype or zoom like crazy.

Multigenerational families are a much trickier logistical issue that would need individualized approaches.

If you are sick, stay home, and certainly do not go to anything COVID ON.

Instead of giving free money to everyone, we figure out how to supplement those in need, those who need support, those we need to protect. Look, I do not have all the answers, but I know this is a way better plan than what we did and are doing.

But again, we need a paradigm shift. We have to shift away from the fear, embrace hope, embrace the possibility of a solution.

Let me give you an example of silly fear. I like watching sports. When they would discuss sports leagues starting up, they were concerned about how they would protect the athletes. From what? They are mostly between the ages of 18-35 and in top shape. I am pretty sure they are safe. Or at least no less safe than they were with the flu and other normal bugs floating around.

Do we remember Michael Jordan playing in the finals with the flu? COVID is less virulent to that age group than the flu. I think they are good.

I have not thought through every situation, but I am confident with all the intelligence and creativity available, we can sort through it. The lies, damn lies, and fake stats created a pandemic of fear that kept us from coming up with the right solution. I think it's time we do.

I will close out this "way forward" section with something from the WHO and Dr. Tedros. He provided this information at a briefing on February 28th, "10 basic things you should know" about COVID.

1. Clean your hands regularly, and don't touch your face.
2. Clean surfaces regularly.
3. Educate yourself on COVID, know the symptoms. "Most people will have mild cases and get better without any special care" and "make sure your information is from reliable sources."
4. Avoid travel if you have a fever or cough.
5. Cough in sleeve or tissue.
6. If you are over 60 or have underlying conditions take extra precautions to avoid crowded areas.
7. If unwell, stay home.
8. If sick, sleep separate from family and use different utensils.
9. If you have trouble breathing, contact your doctor immediately.
10. Being anxious is normal, discuss safety with family and others.

This list is a pretty solid plan and the way we should have proceeded. That was a good job, Dr. Tedros. If we had stuck to this, we would have avoided a lot of self-inflicted damage.

He added a few things at the end of the list.

"Containment starts with you."

"Our greatest enemy is not the virus itself; it is fear, rumors, and stigma. And our greatest assets are facts, reason, and solidarity."

These sentiments were also excellent. And, this is what the "WHO experts" were saying we should do to mitigate COVID as of February 28.

Trump's rally took place later that same day. Trump says, "hoax," compares COVID to flu, and everything changed.

1. Trump is bad and dangerous.
2. Trump is minimizing COVID by comparing it to the flu.
3. Minimizing COVID and comparing it to the flu is bad and dangerous.
4. We must expose that COVID is bad and way worse than the flu to prove that Trump is bad and dangerous.

Four days later, Dr. Tedros gave his fake stats.

On February 28th, Dr. Tedros said, "**our greatest enemy is not the virus itself; it is fear, rumors, and stigma. And our greatest assets are facts, reason, and solidarity.**"

On March 3rd, he gave **false facts** that led to **unreasonable solutions based upon fear** partially created by his **false facts**. What happened Dr. Tedros? You became an unreliable source of information you warned us about in your list.

If you do not believe this is political, simply look at who is "resisting" opening things up. Use your own eyes.

COVID was always going to do its damage. But our greatest enemy and the one that did the most damage was the *FEAR-19 Pandemic* created by hatred for Trump and green journalism.

Hate is poison. Hatred always causes terrible consequences.

Dr. Martin Luther King said,

"Darkness cannot drive out darkness; only light can do that. Hate cannot drive out hate; only love can do that."

We miss you, Dr. King. I wish there were more leaders like you today.

Closing Statement

COVID-19 is terrible; it is highly contagious and kills with devastating precision in our older population. The final death toll is some time off, but I am praying it does not end up anywhere near the 1957 or 1968 flu.

As of this writing, we are at 350,000 deaths worldwide, which is a horrific number. There seems to be a slow decline, but we will have to wait and see. The lockdowns were a variable which makes it harder to predict. We can all hope for the best while we work to protect those who need to be protected.

My objective in writing this book was to show how we allowed politics and green journalism to take a horrible situation and make it much, much worse. I believe that part of the story was completely avoidable.

The press failed in its obligation to ensure that they are giving us factual information. And I fear that nothing is going to change because there is zero chance they will take responsibility for that. They will simply continue to do what it is they do.

That puts it back on us. At some point, we have to decide to stand up and insist that our leaders, our press, and our governments regain trust. I wish I knew how we could go about that; I do not. All I can do is try to help.

There are a ton of other parts to this story, but I could not pull on every thread. My primary focus was to illuminate how and why things escalated to the point they did. The story is a long way from over.

If interested, feel free to find me on _www.thedifferentanimal.com_. I hope to continue trying to help, but I am not sure what form that will take at this time.

Before I close, I have one more tidbit.

The CDC released a report yesterday, May 25th, with updated statistics on COVID. I thought about adding the information back into the completed sections but decided to just include it here at the end.

In their report, they identified their "current best estimate" at the mortality rate of symptomatic infections from COVID at 0.4%. But that is just symptomatic infections, that is still not infection mortality.

They are projecting a current rate of 35% asymptomatic infections. That leaves a current **infection mortality rate of 0.26%.**

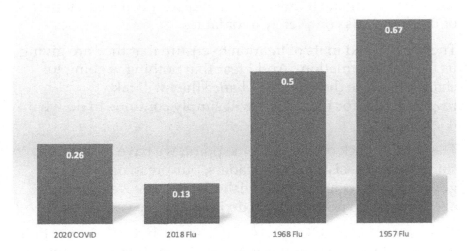

The report includes data received by the CDC before April 29th, 2020.

I have told you over and over that this always comes down. The CDC is already at 0.26%, and that is with data from the end of April. I believe the 35% asymptomatic rate will go up significantly as they explore more.

For instance, the CCMID released the report on May 6th, after the April 29th cutoff date for the CDC report. We talked about it earlier when discussing the Diamond Princess cruise ship. In that study, they determined the asymptomatic rate on the ship was 75%, with a population that averaged 60 years of age.

If the asymptomatic rate goes to 75%, that will make the infection mortality rate for COVID 0.1%. Do you recognize that number? Yea, that is the mortality rate for a "traditional" year of the flu.

I believe the number of asymptomatic will end up higher based upon the ages on the ship and the asymptomatic studies we discussed. Those studies have the number coming in around 90%. That would move the infection mortality rate for COVID at 0.04%. You know, very close to what that controversial Stanford study said.

I have been telling you; the rate will continue to go down.

The COVID boogie man was always a myth. But the effects of the battle with their mythical monster were real.

FINAL, FINAL WORD

The final editing was complete and prepared to go to print. And I saw an article on Buzzfeed this morning, May 29th. Had to add. Sorry if this is less clear because my editor did not clean it up.

I will just give you their opening paragraph.

> New CDC estimates of coronavirus death rates look suspiciously low and present almost no data to back them up, say public health experts who are concerned that the agency is buckling under political pressure to restart the economy.

Wait, wait, I have to include this as well because it's funny. They got a random biostatistician from Florida and a guy from the renowned University of Wollongong to challenge the CDC information.

> "Surely the worst-case scenario should at least be New York for the whole country," said Gideon Meyerowitz-Katz, an epidemiologist at the University of Wollongong in Australia, who has been tracking infection fatality rates in New York City and elsewhere.
>
> And Natalie Dean, a University of Florida biostatistician, said, "The point is that you [should] capture a range of scenarios based on what data we have available right now. With the data we have available right now, we can't rule out something higher. A worst-case scenario needs to be a real worst-case scenario."

I mean, were all the social psychologists busy that day?

Yea, they are pretty invested in their COVID boogie man. Maybe the CDC should apologize.

Look, they are going to continue to argue and defend their boogie man because reason does not matter. The best part is that Buzzfeed uses the updated numbers from New York City in their argument as to why the CDC number is too small.

They point out that the worst numbers in the United States were in New York City, so that should be at least the worst-case scenario in the CDC report. The number they use for New York City is 0.86%. I am guessing they are including those "probable" COVID deaths in their calculations. I am not even going to get into that.

My point is that the worst number in the United States they identify of 0.86% is still lower than the "ten times more lethal than the flu" number of 1%. They were telling us 3, 5, 7, and even 10% mortality at some points. But now, they are arguing it is still terrible because the **worst** case was 0.86%.

The politics of COVID caused the majority of the damage, not COVID. Period. End of Book.

References

Adam Payne, Business Insider, May 21, 2020, A new Swedish coronavirus antibody study suggests the herd-immunity strategy isn't working. Retrieved from: **https://www.businessinsider.com/coronavirus-antibody-study-suggests-sweden-not-reaching-herd-immunity-2020-5**

Alexander Danvers, Psychology Today, May 3, 2020, Does Stanford Owe us and Apology for that COVID-19 Study? Retrieved from: **https://www.psychologytoday.com/intl/blog/how-do-you-know/202005/does-stanford-owe-us-apology-covid-19-study**

Alice Miranda Ollstein, Politico, February 2, 2020, Coronavirus Quanteen, Travel Ban could backfire, experts fear. Retieved from: **https://www.politico.com/news/2020/02/04/coronavirus-quaratine-travel-110750**

Allison Aubrey, NRP, January 29, 2020. Worried About Catching The New Coronavirus? In the U.S., Flu Is A Bigger Threat. Retrieved from: **https://www.npr.org/sections/health-shots/2020/01/29/800813299/worried-about-catching-the-new-coronavirus-in-the-u-s-flu-is-a-bigger-threat**

Amy Hollyfield, ABC7 News, May 21, 2020, Suicides on the rise amid stay-at-home order, Bay Area medical professionals say. Retrieved from: **https://abc7news.com/suicide-covid-19-coronavirus-rates-during-pandemic-death-by/6201962/**

Amy Mitchell, Jeffrey Gottfried, Galen Stocking, Katerina Eva Matsa, Elizabeth Grieco, Pew Research Center, October 2, 2017, Covering President Trump in a Polarized Media Environment. Retrieved from: **https://www.journalism.org/2017/10/02/covering-president-trump-in-a-polarized-media-environment/?utm_content=bufferc900b&utm_medium=social&utm_source=twitter.com&utm_campaign=buffer**

Andrew Harnik, AP, October 18, 2016, Journalists Shower Hillary Clinton With Campaign Cash. Retrieved from: **https://publicintegrity.org/politics/journalists-shower-hillary-clinton-with-campaign-cash/**

Anthony S. Fauci, M.D., H. Clifford Lane, M.D., and Robert R. Redfield, M.D., New England Journal of Medicine, February 28, 2020, COVID-19 – Navigating the Uncharted. Retrieved from: **https://www.nejm.org/doi/full/10.1056/NEJMe2002387**

Ashley Abramson, APA, April 8, 2020. How COVID-19 may increase domestic violence and child abuse. Retrived from: **https://www.apa.org/topics/covid-19/domestic-violence-child-abuse**

Bandy X. Lee, USA Today, Oct. 11, 2019. Mental health experts see Trump is dangerous, but our professional gatekeepers protect him. Reviewed from: **https://www.usatoday.com/story/opinion/voices/2019/10/11/donald-trump-mentally-unfit-american-psychiatric-association-column/3917647002/**

Ben Conarck, Daniel Chang, Miami Herald, April 24, 2020, Miami-Dade has tens of thousands of missed coronavirus infections, UM survey finds. Retrieved from: **https://www.miamiherald.com/news/coronavirus/article242260406.html**

Bernadette Hogan and Julia Marsh, MY Post, March 27, 2020, Coronavirus in NY: Cuomo defends need for 30K ventilators after Trump called it overblown. Retrieved from: **https://nypost.com/2020/03/27/coronavirus-in-ny-cuomo-defends-need-for-30k-ventilators-after-trump-called-it-overblown/**

Brian Resnick, VOX, March 13, 2020. COVID-19 is not the flu, it's worse. Retrieved from: **https://www.vox.com/science-and-health/2020/3/13/21176735/covid-19-coronavirus-worse-than-flu-comparison**

CCDC Weekly, Vital Surveillance: The Epidemiological Characteristics of an Outbreak of 2019 Novel Coronavirus Diseases (COVID-19)-China, 2020. Retrieved from: **http://weekly.chinacdc.cn/en/article/id/e53946e2-c6c4-41e9-9a9b-fea8db1a8f51**

CDC.gov

CDC.gov, May 25th, 2020, COVID-19 Pandemic Planning Scenarios. Retrieved from: **https://www.cdc.gov/coronavirus/2019-ncov/hcp/planning-scenarios.html**

Cecelia Smith-Schoenwalder, US News and World Report, Jan. 30, 2020, Why the Flu Is Still a Bigger COVID-19 Projections, New York. Retrieved from: **https://covid19.healthdata.org/united-states-of-america/new-york**

Children's Bureau, March 2019, Child Abuse and Neglect Fatalities 2017: Statistics. Retrieved from: **https://www.childwelfare.gov/pubPDFs/fatality.pdf**

CNBC, February 28, 2020, World Health Organization holds news conference on the coronavirus outbreak. Retrieved from: **https://www.youtube.com/watch?v=G23drPPjxMY&t=841s**

Deena Beasley, Kristina Cooke, Rueters, April 14, 2020, New York City hospitals cancal termporary workers as coronavirus cases stabilize. Retrieved from: **https://www.reuters.com/article/us-health-coronavirus-newyork-staffing-idUSKCN21X00X**

Cecelia Smith-Schoenwalder, US News and World Report, Jan 30, 2020, Why the Flu is Still a Bigger Threat to Americans Than Coronavirus. Retrieved from: **https://www.usnews.com/news/health-news/articles/2020-01-30/why-the-flu-is-a-bigger-threat-to-the-us-than-coronavirus**

David K. Li, NBC News, March 23, 2020. New York Death Toll Crosses 15,000 with probably cases. Retieved from: **https://www.nbcnews.com/health/health-news/live-blog/2020-04-23-coronavirus-news-n1190201/ncrd1191146#blogHeader**

David Montgomery, NPR News, March 11, 2020. COVID-19, How it Compares to other Diseases in Five Charts. Retrieved from: **https://www.mprnews.org/story/2020/03/11/covid19-how-it-compares-with-other-diseases-in-5-charts**

Don Moore, Yahoo, March 26, 2020, Trump's overconfidence has always been dangerous. With coronavirus, it's deadly. Retrieved from: **https://news.yahoo.com/op-ed-trumps-overconfidence-always-100020361.html**

Dr. Viniyak Kumar, ABC News, March 27, 2020. COVID-19 had been compared to the flu. Experts say that is wrong. Retrieved from: **https://abcnews.go.com/Health/covid-19-compared-flu-experts-wrong/story?id=69779116**

Eran Bendavid, Bianca Mulaney, Neeraj Sood, Soleil Shah, Emilia Ling, Rebecca Bromley-Dulfano, Cara Lai, Zoe Weissberg, Rodrigo Saavedra-Walker, James Tedrow, Dona Tversky, Andrew Bogan, Thomas Kupiec, Daniel Eichner, Pibhav Gupta, John Ioannidis, Jay Bhattacharya, April 30, 2020, medRxiv, COVID-19 Antibody Seroprevalence in Santa Clara County, California. Revtieved from: **https://www.medrxiv.org/content/10.1101/2020.04.14.20062463v2**

Global News, Feb 26, 2020 Coronavirus outbreak: Donald Trump, CDC addresses US Preparedness for possible COVID-19 threat. Retieved from: **https://www.youtube.com/watch?v=Wi35088F1Ns**

Greg Norman, Fox News, April 23, 2020. Nearly 3 Million New Yorkers have had coronavirus, antibody study suggests. Retrieved from: **https://www.foxnews.com/us/new-york-antibody-study-early-results**

Gregory Burns, Harvard Business Press, September 2, 2008, Iconoclast: A neuroscientist reveals how to think differently.

—

Holly Secon, Business Insider, March 30, 2020. The coronavirus death rate in the US is far higher than that of the flu – here's how the 2 compare across age ranges." Retrieved from: **https://www.businessinsider.com/coronavirus-compared-seasonal-flu-in-the-us-death-rates-2020-3**

Huffington Post, March 9, 2019, HuffPost: Democratic Primary. Retrieved from: **https://big.assets.huffingtonpost.com/athena/files/2020/03/09/5e66602ec5 b68d6164581ea9.pdf**

Jessica Jones, Reuters, May 13, 2020, Spanish antibody study points to 5% of population affected by conronvirus. Reviewed from: **https://www.reuters.com/article/us-health-coronavirus-spain-study-idUSKBN22P2RP**

Jon C Emery, Timothy W Russell, Yang Liu, Joel Hellewell, Carl A.B. Pearson, CMMID nCov working group, Gwen Knight, Rosalind M Eggo, Adam J Kucharski, Sebastian Funk, Stehan Flasche, and Rein M G J Houben, CMMID, May 5th, 2020. The contribution of asymptomatic SARS-CoV-2 infections to transmission – a model-based analysis of the Diamond Princess outbreak. Retrieved from: **https://cmmid.github.io/topics/covid19/asymp-transmission.html?utm_source=miragenews&utm_medium=miragenew s&utm_campaign=news**

Kaylee Hartung, Michael Mendelsohn, Matthew Fuhrman, Enjoli Francis, ABC News, April 20, 2020. Antibody test study results suggest COVID-19 cases likely much higher than reported. Retrieved from: **https://abcnews.go.com/Health/results-antibody-test-study-reveal-covid-19-cases/story?id=70249753**

Kieran Corcoran, Business Insider, April 19, 2020, A test of 200 people just outside Boston found that 32% had been exposed to the coronavirus compared to official rate of 2%. Retrieved from: **https://www.businessinsider.com/coronavirus-test-200-chelsea-massachusetts-finds-32-percent-exposed-2020-4**

Kevin Liptak, Maegan Vazquez, Nick Valencia, Jim Acosta, CNN, March. 24, 2020, Trump says he wants the country 'opened up and just raring to go by Easter,' despite health experts' warnings. Retrieved from: **https://www.cnn.com/2020/03/24/politics/trump-easter-economy-coronavirus/index.html**

Lenny Bernstein, Washington Post, February 1, 2020, Get a grippe, America. The flu is a much bigger threat than coronavirus, for now. https://www.washingtonpost.com/health/time-for-a-reality-check-america-the-flu-is-a-much-bigger-threat-than-coronavirus-for-now/2020/01/31/46a15166-4444-11ea-b5fc-eefa848cde99_story.html

Matthew Yglesias, VOX, May 16, 2020, The results of a Spanish study on COVID-19 immunity have a scary takeaway. Retrieved from: https://www.vox.com/2020/5/16/21259492/covid-antibodies-spain-serology-study-coronavirus-immunity

Mediabiasfactcheck.com

Megan Henry and Grace Hauck, USA Today, February 1, 2020, Coronavirus is scary, but the flu is deadlier, more widespread. Retieved from: https://www.usatoday.com/story/news/health/2020/02/01/coronavirus-flu-deadlier-more-widespread-than-wuhan-china-virus/4632508002/

MSNBC, March 16, 2020, Trump gave Republicans false hope on coronavirus. Retieved from: https://www.msnbc.com/the-last-word/watch/lawrence-trump-gave-republicans-false-hope-on-coronavirus-80752197624

MSNBC, March 9, 2020, Trump Compared Coronavirus to the flu. Here's why that's a bad idea. Retrieved from: https://www.youtube.com/watch?v=zG4d2kd-NKc

MSNBC, March 29, 2020, Confirmed COVID-19 cases surpass 120,000; more than 2,000 deaths.

National Institute of Infectious Disease: Field Briefing: Diamond Princess Covid-19 Classes, 20 Feb Update. Retrieved from: https://www.niid.go.jp/niid/en/2019-ncov-e/9417-covid-dp-fe-02.html

NBC News, March 11, 2020, Coronavirus Expert Dr. Fauci, CDC Director Dr. Redfield Testify. Retrieved from: https://www.youtube.com/watch?v=RsqUve07HcA

NYC Health, COVID-19 Data. Retrieved from: https://www1.nyc.gov/site/doh/covid/covid-19-data.page

obhwfgirl, urbandictionary.com, August 8, 2007, Green Journalism. Retrieved from: https://www.urbandictionary.com/define.php?term=green%20journalism

Peter Barlow, Medical Express, December 23, 2019. Can you die from the common cold? Retrieved from: https://medicalxpress.com/news/2019-12-die-common-cold.html

Peter William Horby, The Lancet, March 17, 2014. Community studies of influenze: new knowledge, new questions. Retrieved from: **https://www.thelancet.com/journals/lanres/article/PIIS2213-2600(14)70053-0/fulltext**

Peter Snarr, Kron4, March 19, 2020. In letter to Trump, Newsom eslitmates 56% of Californians will be infected with coronavirus. Retrieved from: **https://www.kron4.com/news/gov-newsom-sends-letter-to-us-congressional-leaders-requesting-additional-financial-assistance-for-coronavirus/**

Sandy Fitzgerald, Newsmax, February 3, 2020, China furious with US on growing travel ban. Retrieved from: **https://www.newsmax.com/headline/china-coronavirus-who-us/2020/02/03/id/952364/**

Sino Bilogical, Hong Kong Flu (1968 Influenza Pandemic). Retrieved from: **https://www.sinobiological.com/research/virus/1968-influenza-pandemic-hong-kong-flu**

Stephanie M. Lee, Dan Vergano, Buzzfeed News, May 28th, 2020, The CDC Released New Death Rate Estimates for the Coronavirus. Many Scientists Say They're Too Low. Retrieved from: **https://www.buzzfeednews.com/article/stephaniemlee/coronavirus-cdc-infection-fatality-rate**

Stephen Collinson, CNN, March 20, 2020, Trump peddles unsubstantiated hope in dark times. Retieved from: **https://www.cnn.com/2020/03/20/politics/donald-trump-coronavirus-false-hope/index.html**

Steven Sternberg, US News and World Report, March 20, 2020, Coronavirus Overshadows a Deadly Flu Season. Retrieved from: **https://www.usnews.com/news/health-news/articles/2020-03-20/coronavirus-pandemic-overshadows-a-deadly-flu-season**

Steve Villano, medium.com, March 26, 2020, Yes, Andrew Cuomo Can Be Nominated for President in 2020. Retrieved from: **https://medium.com/@stevevillano/yes-andrew-cuomo-can-be-nominated-for-president-in-2020-777715997771**

Taylor Romine, CNN, April 17, 2020. 'We need to fix it quickly.' Asymptomatic coronavirus cases at Boston homeless shelter raise red flag. Retrieved from: **https://www.cnn.com/2020/04/17/us/boston-homeless-coronavirus-outbreak/index.html**

Timothy W Russell, Joel Hellewell, Christopher I Jarvis, Kevin van-Zandervoort, Sam Abbott, Ruwan Ratnayake, CMMID nCov working group, Stehan Flasche, Fosalind M Eggo, Adam J Kucharski, medRxiv, Estimating the infection and case fatality ratio for COVID-19 using age adjusted data from the outbreak on the Diamond Princess cruise ship. Retrieved from: **https://www.medrxiv.org/content/10.1101/2020.03.05.20031773v2**

UbuntuFM, Medium, Dec. 2, 2017, THE FOURTH ESTATE – On the role of journalism: facts vs. fake news. Retrieved from: **https://medium.com/@ubuntufm/the-fourth-estate-on-the-role-of-journalism-facts-vs-fake-news-61168f8e8cf**

United Nations, March 2, 2020, Coronavirus Outbreak (COVID – 19): WHO Update. Retrieved from: **https://www.youtube.com/watch?v=-kk-DrTCRAY**

Veronica Morley, 23ABC News, April 27, 2020. YouTube issues statement of removal of controversial video interview with Bakersfield doctors. Retrieved from: **https://www.turnto23.com/news/coronavirus/video-interview-with-dr-dan-erickson-and-dr-artin-massihi-taken-down-from-youtube**

William Wan, Washington Post, May 4, 2020, The coronavirus pandemic is pushing America into a mental health crisis. Retrieved from: **https://www.washingtonpost.com/health/2020/05/04/mental-health-coronavirus/**

Washington Post Editorial Board, March 25, 2020, Trump is spreading false hope for a virus cure – and that's not the only damage. Retrieved from: **https://www.washingtonpost.com/opinions/global-opinions/trump-is-spreading-false-hope-for-a-virus-cure--and-thats-not-the-only-damage/2020/03/25/587b26d8-6ec3-11ea-b148-e4ce3fbd85b5_story.html**

World Health Organization, February 3, 2020, WHO Director-General Dr. Tedros address to the 146th Session of the Executive Board. Retrieved from: **https://www.youtube.com/watch?v=SIT8fvHUDDE**

Made in the USA
Middletown, DE
31 July 2020

14110397R00066